All the best!

Cathy Snedgne

It Is What It Is, Or Is It....

All About Business

Jeff Roziere,
Cathy Snelgrove

ISBN: 978-1-4772-6934-3 (sc)
ISBN: 978-1-4772-6935-0 (hc)
ISBN: 978-1-4772-6933-6 (e)

About the Authors

Jeff and Cathy spent the early part of their careers in executive management positions with a number of Fortune 500, publically traded, private corporations, and government organizations.

After starting DiscoverYou, they worked with and challenged numerous small- to medium-sized business leaders and owners to create outstanding business results in their companies. Their diverse experience in operations, sales, human resources, lean, and safety systems allows them to bring a unique perspective to the ins and outs of running a business in changing times. Combining a knowledge of human psychology with what it takes to generate peak performance, they leave their clients always asking for more.

Visit www.discoveryou.me for more information

It Is What It Is, Or Is It... All About Business....

A must read if you want to take charge of your thinking. Jeff and Cathy illustrate the phases of thinking in relation to the business life cycle and then challenge you to confront your conventions and models of the world on the way to creating impressive business performance.

J. Watt, B. Sc., MBA, CHRP

It Is What It Is, Or Is It... All About Business....

After reading this book, it only stands to reason why Jeff and Cathy have been so successful in generating real value for their clients and students.

M. Linklater, www.DLSafeMoney.com

It Is What It Is, Or Is It... All About Business....

As I read this book I began to open a new world of performance at a level I never thought possible. I was amazed at how easy it all became when I worked with the cycles to create growth.

C. Griffin, President, Alternative Landscaping Ltd.

It Is What It Is, Or Is It... All About Business....

Is a book that I gift to my friends and colleagues. It has not only impacted my performance in my business, but in other areas of my life. This is way too valuable to keep it a secret from those you care about.

T. Sandruski, B. Sc., MBA

Table of Contents

Introduction· ·1

The Convention of Business ·9

The Model — Part One· 23

The Model — Part Two· ·37

The Pendulum Swing· ·51

There Is Certainty Only in Uncertainty· · · · · · · · · · · · · · · · ·65

Problems versus Opportunities ·77

Fear· ·89

Holding Your Intention ·101

Conclusion ·113

End Notes· ·121

Introduction

We believe success in business or in anything is simply all in your mind. You create performance, based on what you are thinking about or how you are interpreting the world in any given moment. Yet so many of us are unaware of what we are actually thinking, moment to moment. To prove this, what were you thinking about five minutes ago? How about thirty minutes ago? How about three minutes ago? There is a constant dialogue going on behind the scenes that we are oblivious to because our focus is caught up in the seemingly important things right here in front of us, in the moment.

A while back, my niece asked me a question about polar bears. She asked me, "If a polar bear was alone in a zoo and had never been in the wild, how would it know that it was a polar bear?" Just think about that for a moment. How would it know? We have asked a lot of people their thoughts and ideas on this seemingly simple question, and there has been a huge range of answers from "maybe it wouldn't know" to "it would inherently know." It is a funny question, because in fact, is this not the same thing that could be said about you? When you were born, how did you know who you were? How do you know who you are today? Could you be more than you yourself realize you are? Who are you to the people around you? Who are you not? How do you know? Have you ever considered what you think you know about you could in fact be wrong, and you are even more than you realize you are now?

So you might ask, "What does this have to do with business?" In fact, it has everything to do with business. As a leader in your organization, these are the questions and thoughts which are constantly at play behind the scenes, and while you are generally unconscious to them, they do govern how you think, how you perform, and ultimately how your company performs.

As you read through the chapters in this book, you will notice that this book is different and is a lot of fun to read, because it is meant to have you look at the world differently. We respect each of you has a vast amount of experience and knowledge, and that has allowed you to get where you are today. We know that you didn't get there by simply sitting idly by and watching the world. There were people who challenged your thinking and ideas, and in doing so, they created new possibilities for you.

Think back to those people who have had the biggest impact on you. Were there times when you didn't want to hear what they were saying? Were there times that they disagreed with you and maybe you were frustrated by them? Were there times when maybe you disregarded them however, what they said still resonates with you today? Could it be they held a greater intention for you?

We hold a belief that individuals are often the hardest on the people that they care about the most. When you think about it, there are numerous things that happen around you, each and every day. You don't even consider them, and you certainly don't talk about them. Why? Simply because they are not important to you. Then there are those people whom you give advice to, even when maybe they don't want to hear it. At times it may be that you push them, when they don't think they want to be pushed. At times, maybe you point out things you think they haven't considered. It is not because you don't care about them. It is not because you don't believe in them. In fact, it is the opposite. You hold a greater intention for them, and you want to see them be the success you know they can be. In reading this book, think of us as you.

We have worked with countless business leaders, in their companies and with them personally, to create performance; they will all attest to how uncomfortable it can be at times. Our focus and intention is around performance and in creating this for ourselves and our clients. For this we make no apologies. You know yourself there are times when people like you want other people to get into their boat with them. How many times have you heard people talk about some sort of problem, and in telling you about it, they are looking to you to tell them that you understand how hard it must all be? If you are one of those individuals who climb in the boat with them, it is funny how often you soon realize that the boat is sinking and you are going down with it in the process. On the other hand, if you are the individual who holds a higher intention for that individual and has him or her recognize a different possibility, not only do you stay out of the boat, but you pull him or her out as well. We always tell the people we are working with that if they are looking for someone to climb in the boat with them, in fact, we are "dry-landers." We respect them too much to climb in with them.

We like to poke fun at the world and at people's models of the world. We are clear you can always come up with some reason, or convenient excuse, to explain why it is you are where you are, or why it is that you are not where you want to be. Have you ever noticed "why" is often the questions that is asked in our general society, and so just in being asked, you have to build some sort of reason to justify it. We see it differently. If people really knew what it was that got them in the spot they are in, then they would fix it or change it if it wasn't working. We never ask "why"; we ask "how did you get there?" What was it in your thinking that created your situation and what would you need to be thinking to create something different? Everyone has an amazing set of tools and resources at their disposal. They sometimes just forget they have them, and because of this, forget how to access them.

We know some of you may have picked up this book expecting us to give you a formula for success. Sorry, we believe it is up to you to create your own formula. You know there is no such thing as a "one size fits all" for success, and if there were, wouldn't everyone have figured it out already? Wouldn't everyone have all they want if this were the case? There are many different books you can pick up; they will all tell you they have the answer, and that if you just follow their instructions, you too will have success. Is this really the case? Sure, there are concepts and ideas that are interpreted and presented to you by the author for your interpretation, which ultimately opens up your thinking and we believe that is fantastic. However, the point is, it is you who needs to make the interpretation that changes your thinking. It is you who needs to go out and apply it. The success you achieved isn't in the book; it is in how it changed your thinking. There is no one recipe for success. We know the recipe for your success is inside you, and whether you realize it or not at this point, you also know how to create it. All you have to do is be open to the possibility.

This book is about challenging your thinking. It is about making you uncomfortable at times, and it is about making you laugh as you realize that something you believed just a moment ago is no longer true. More importantly, this journey is about opening you up to question the things you see and hear around you and to have you become aware of the

3

unconscious thinking that is creating your current level of performance. Whether you realize it or not, just by reading these first few words, you have started down a path that will change your world forever. When you think of that, isn't it exciting? You see, simply stated, you can't un-know something once you know it, no matter how hard you try.

Think of your mind as computer software or a computer program. When a new version of software is launched, the developer believes that it is capable of providing something amazing. Once it hits the users and the users start to use it, they provide feedback to the developer. The developer recognizes that maybe there are some bugs, and he goes and fixes those and then launches an update. At some point, the developer realizes that if she did a little tweaking here and there, the program would be even more powerful. So once she does, then she launches either a new version or an update, and the cycle continues. If those developers were not constantly seeking new possibilities for their products or if they didn't fix the bugs in the program, how long do you think it would take their program to become unusable? We would think, not very long. Our minds are the same. They constantly need to be updated and stimulated in exciting ways, and when they are not, they get tired and bored. We also know at times, old programs need to be uninstalled, for new opportunities to be installed.

We know you understand this, because you are reading this. There are many people around us who think that we are a little crazy, and to tell you the truth, we like to be a little crazy. You see, crazy gets results. Everyone says they go the extra mile, although the extra mile can be a lonely place. Most people, once they get there, realize there is no one else there and they leave, never to return again. However, for the few who go there and choose to stay there, they realize it doesn't take long to find other people who like to be there as well. That is also why the extra mile is a place filled with opportunities. It is the same as a little crazy. It can be a little lonely at first, but it doesn't take long before others show up and want to join in on the fun. How many people around you are "normal" and unhappy, bored, or unfulfilled? How about you? Are you ready to try out the extra mile and be a little crazy?

In this book, we want to introduce you to some different ideas around the convention of business. We will poke some fun around "Who says?" that will have you question some of what you have been told about business and the world in general. You will begin to notice some of the rules, which you might think apply to everyone, in fact are different for some. In the following chapters, we introduce some different thinking around the inevitability of cycles in business, and will use the business and product / service life cycles as the premise to do this. While there are those who work diligently to fight these cycles, there are those who have learned to work with them, and in doing so, create performance for themselves. A cycle is driven by a pendulum swing in thinking, and you will learn how to look at things differently in terms of these momentums. Finally, we will introduce a number of different concepts that will fundamentally change your thought process and how you look at the world:

- The only thing you can be certain of is uncertainty.
- Problems and opportunities are constructed the same way.
- Fear is just a construct, and it is not real.
- Your intention, your focus, is the only thing that will create your success.

Early on in my career, I worked for The Boeing Company as a senior manufacturing manager, overseeing a portion of the operations in one of the plants. At the time, we were considered to be a small plant, and there was always a focus on reducing costs and cycle time in the operation in order to remain competitive. The cycle time through my shops was approximately twenty-four days, and we were getting prepared to do a workshop focused on making reductions in that time. I was fortunate to have the opportunity to work with an outside advisor named Bill.

The first day we met, we agreed to establish some goals the group would achieve throughout the workshop. When Bill asked me what I thought the cycle-time target should be, I said twenty-one days, to which he replied, "How about three?" At first, I thought we were on the same page. Twenty-four minus three got us to twenty-one days. After a second or two, he clarified, "No, I mean three days in total." I remembered thinking that he obviously didn't know our system and that he didn't know what we had to deal with. My team and I took him for a tour of the operation, and when we got back to the room, he asked me, "So, what do you think the target should be?" and I replied that I thought that we might be able to get to eighteen, to which he replied, "How about three?" Throughout that afternoon, we went back and forth. The team would show him more data, he would ask the question, to which we would give him a lower number - fifteen, fourteen, ten, to which he would always reply, "How about three?" In the end, after the team had gone home for the day, we still seemed to be at a stalemate.

I had thoughts that maybe there was something he knew that I didn't. It was troubling in he seemed so confident in his target, and in the moment, there was no way I could ever see being able to reach it. The funny thing was that as we were winding up for the day, I noticed he had a beautiful Lacrosse pen and pencil set in front of him; those who know me, know I love pen and pencil sets. You know those times when you say something and you wish, the second you said it, you could somehow grab the words and put them back in your mouth? Well, this was one of those times. Next thing you know, I said, "Tell you what, Bill, if we make it to three days, I want your pen and pencil set," to which he replied, "It's a deal!"

As soon as I realized what I had agreed to, there was an incredible amount of fear. What was I going to tell the three hundred people working for me? They would think that I had gone crazy. Where were we going to start? What was my boss going to think when we didn't make it? How could I have ever agreed to such a thing, over a stupid pen and pencil set? I remember all the way through the process of that six-month project, he pushed us to push our thinking. He held an intention higher than any of us could have held for ourselves, right from the start. He was unwavering in his belief and his focus around meeting our goal. He didn't come with a bunch of answers or ideas. He didn't need to. All he had to do was to believe that we had them.

This brings us back to the polar bear. How would he know he was a polar bear if no one told him? What have you been told about running a business? What have you been told about solving problems? What have you been told about operating in your market and how it needs to be done? What have you been told in terms of creating something different? More importantly, what do you believe? Do you believe you are a polar bear because someone told you that you have a white fur coat, so you are? If that were the case, could you not be a rabbit? Do you believe you are a polar bear because someone told you, because you growl, you are? If that were the case, could you not be a lion? What do you really think about you as a leader and about your business? If you want to have some fun, write down a few notes, and then compare them to your thinking at the end of this book. Notice how much change you make in your thinking, just in reading a book, and think about what else is in store for you as you continue on the path.

Here is the very first point we want to make and for you to think about as you continue on. You are the only one who is in charge of your thinking. Just think about this for a moment. The last time we checked, there was no one who has the ability to go into your head and make you think something you don't want to think. You ultimately have the choice, and we encourage you to choose the thinking that is right for you, because what you think really does impact your results.

The Convention of Business

Growth-related challenges are identified as the most common issue facing small- to medium-sized businesses today. Business, in general, views a quickly evolving, changing, and uncertain economic and global climate as a moving target. As witness to this, many companies are struggling to stay alive, never mind realize the potential growth that is available to them. The challenges facing business are present not only in the United States and Canada. Many of these same challenges are faced by every small- to medium-sized business around the world. In the United States and Canada, there is an abundance of data and statistics that provide a context to the issues.

In the United States, the consumer over the past four years has tightened spending. People remain either underemployed or unemployed, and small- to medium-sized businesses, in many areas, continue to struggle to remain afloat. In Canada, though the market has remained relatively positive in comparison to the United States, these same challenges remain. According to Industry Canada and COMPAS, the following issues were identified as the critical barriers to growth for the small- to medium-sized business sectors:

- 73 percent identify keeping or retaining valued employees as important,
- 62 percent identify training and skills development as important,
- 58 percent identify recruiting new employees with the skills needed as important,
- 57 percent identify government regulation and the cost of compliance as important, and
- 52 percent identify access to financing and capital as important.[1]

Business at its basic level can be broken down into four main areas: Finance, Marketing, Human Resources, and Operations. It is of little surprise the issues identified above stem from each of the four areas of business. Of great interest is the fact that access to financing and capital was rated lowest of these needs, while to listen to the media, this would be considered one of the greatest hurdles to building business today.

Capital and finance are the driving forces behind business, for without them, you essentially have no business. Perhaps part of the reason for this oversight is the fact that they are also the least understood aspect of small- to medium-sized business, and therefore they often do not receive the attention that the others do.

It is human nature to focus on areas of "personal strength" when working to address the "perceived" problems in any area. In fact, there are business gurus who have made a killing beating the "strengths" drum. We see the world a little differently, as you will learn throughout this book. It is our view that most of the population put their focus on logical systems and systemic reasons for issues, instead of understanding how they themselves construct a problem or opportunity and, as such, find little resolve. True adepts, the very few, understand the opportunity that exists within the structure of a problem. Many speak of it; however, few experience and live by it. You will notice those who seem to quietly go about running their business and make it seem effortless. They are almost unnoticed at times, and then suddenly they take over an industry or a sector before anyone recognized they were there. The vast majority of the population speaks of luck and timing for those success stories, but is this really the case, or is it that they understand the world differently?

Warren Buffet, once said, "Be fearful when others are greedy, be greedy when others are fearful." These simple words hold a tremendous amount of insight into the world of business. Many hear it and acknowledge it; however for many, it is hard to get their heads around it and even harder to actualize it. In our society, including business, we are continually in a cycle of highs and lows. Truth be told, it is never as good as you think it is, nor as bad as you think and here is why. People in general operate and behave as if they are part of a herd, and they possess that same herd mentality. This is not meant to be derogatory by any means; it is just a natural part of how most operate. On the one hand, this is what creates everyone running for the doors when they hear the economy is struggling. At the same time, if there wasn't such a thing, we wouldn't have mass marketing, there wouldn't be millions of Crocs being sold each year, and you wouldn't be able to sell to as many customers as you do.

In general, we like to live by rules, so that we don't really have to think too much. They give us a level of certainly, and it can appear that "There is safety in numbers." The second thing, though, with this herd mentality is there is the propensity to focus only on the here and now inside the confines of the rules. You see, when we look out, we construct problems in the here and now that get in the way of us looking out, and it can create a vicious cycle - one that is difficult to break.

If we look once again at the business challenges outlined previously, they highlight this type of focus that a herd of business leaders may take on over a period of time. In many cases, business leaders, in fact, are not experiencing these problems today, and that is why we can find stories and statistics that counteract the data. There are companies that are successful and are flourishing in this economy, so is it they are doing something different, or is it they don't buy into the mind-set that inflicts so many others? We believe in the latter, and as you read on, you will too. In reality, we are all operating in the same environment, with the same challenges; however, some have learned to stretch their thinking in a different way, and in doing so, are finding results.

At a Canadian Manufacturers and Exporters Conference in 2001, business leaders in manufacturing had gathered and were speaking of similar challenges facing their businesses. At the time, addressing skilled labor shortages and the adoption of lean manufacturing practices were being thrown around as requirements for meeting the challenges of the future. At the time, the Canadian dollar was trading around 68 cents relative to the US dollar, and the Canadian manufacturers were reaping massive benefit due to the exchange. Companies were extremely optimistic, and sales were steadily increasing into the US market. The flavor of the conference was prosperity and meeting demand. In one of the breakout groups, a CEO from a small energy company posed a contrary idea to the group. He warned, "In the future, if your margins are based solely on the currency trade, your profits will decline, and your company will fail over the next ten years." Largely the group, while focused on their own prosperity in the here and now, scoffed at the speaker. Ten short years later, we have in essence a par dollar, and we are sure there are those who wondered how he could have predicted that. In short, his thinking was different.

Oftentimes, when we work with leaders, we find they place problems outside of themselves. They get caught up in the convenient excuses of the herd mentality for their lack of growth. They get caught in a cycle of thinking. Less than 10 percent, in our estimation, understand their true intentions and what the convention of business truly stands for. These are the leaders who understand the organization or business is a reflection of their own thinking and focus and that it is simply a tool to actualize their own intention. Then there are those who believe their company is a reflection of the economy or of their market, or something else that they perceive to have limited control over. As you will learn, when you put something outside of you, it becomes a convenient excuse you hang your hat on, however it doesn't yield performance or results.

Everybody knows that there is a convention to business. It is what we teach to our business students. It is what we fall back on when we look to solve problems or to go after opportunities. In fact, there are numerous industries and companies that have been spawned to support these ideas and concepts. They are the rules that we adopt to help us to operate. In order to fully understand how to begin to think in a way that will change your company, you must first know the opposite side of the equation. Let's explore the convention in business, and as you read this, think about how it could restrict your thinking.

For this purpose, let's agree business is comprised of four main areas: Finance, Marketing, Human Resources, and Operations. Business is simply a system, in and of itself, so we know each area impacts and is impacted by the others, throughout the various levels of connectivity. What we mean is that *finance* could be said to be the lifeblood of your business. It is capital that drives new product or service growth and innovation. It is the cash flow and profit that keep the company operational. Money is the backbone that drives an organization. Finance drives *marketing*, a process that takes a company's product or service to select markets for exchange and drives the perceived need for the company's product or services. Finance drives *human resources* as a secondary capital that embodies a company's knowledge, abilities, and ultimate success. The people capital is the conduit, utilizing other resources such as equipment and processes to translate an idea into a tangible product or service. Finally, finance drives the *operations* or processes that drive the feeding of the product or service to the end user. When all are in balance, they drive profit back into the organization, thereby feeding the system of business. This is convention. In general, most of you will agree with us this is how business operates; and as soon as a group believes something to be true, it in fact becomes convention.

Alone, each area can be complex in nature, and over the years, business minds, educators, economists, business leaders, and so on have worked to develop the ultimate equation for business success. We have all developed rules and governing laws in each area in order to attempt to predict how each of these will impact the overall business system. Today, the convention around each of these areas can be one of debate. We are constantly learning and evaluating, so as new ideas and thoughts come into play, sometimes we find that what we thought we knew at one time no longer holds true.

Case in point: the introduction of the Internet has had a dramatic impact on the advertising portion of the marketing industry. Not that long ago, in order to market a product, you simply needed to position your product on a shelf at the general store. Today, we reach consumers with Google and Facebook Ads, product positioning in movies and television shows, search engine queries, e-mail traffic, blogs, and so on. Advertising today has a marked difference over even what existed as convention five years ago, yet many business leaders continue to hold the premise of the convention that existed yesterday.

For a moment, let's look a little deeper inside an example of conventional thinking in business in terms of the life cycle of business and the life cycle of products or services. Now, we know that you will agree with us that people are constantly changing, and as their values transition, so do their needs and wants. Business cycles and product or service life cycles transition and change in conjunction with the natural desires of the people they serve. Those businesses that are able to change and adapt in their models are the ones that remain relevant and viable. To bring some context to this, think about how we parent our children. How you parent your children at infancy is different from how you parent them as teenagers; your role changes as they become adults. It has to evolve in support of their needs, and if it doesn't, you become stifled in your relationship with them. Similarly your business and the management of it will follow a similar changing cycle. How you operate your business during start-up is different from how you may run it today.

Numerous experts have written that there are four phases to the business cycle and the product or service life cycle. We have noticed that when you combine them, they have a similar thread of thinking, although they are often explained as separate models.

- Product / service and business have a limited life,
- Product / service sales and business pass through distinct stages, each consisting of different challenges, opportunities, and problems for the leader to maneuver through,
- Products and business require different marketing, financing, manufacturing, purchasing, operation, and human resource strategies in each life cycle stage; and
- The length of time associated with each phase is dependent on the product / service or the business.

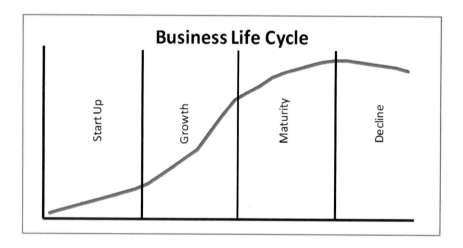

By agreeing that the four phases shown above exist, there are other things we are certain that we know. For example, Experts in the business field have reached a consensus that:

In the *Start Up Phase*, costs associated with the company and products are very high, coupled with slower sales volumes early on. Often in the case of new business, products or services have little or no competition in the market. The company in this stage is responsible for creating the needs and wants (demand) for the product. Companies are required to work with the target markets to prompt the use of their products. In this phase, the company is on its way to the growth phase; however, in this phase, usually company profits are very small or nonexistent.

In the *Growth Phase*, cost reductions occur based on the economies of scale, while sales volumes increase significantly. The marrying of these two principles increases the profitability of the company. Overall awareness of the company and product / services is on the rise, and the target markets are now aware of the offerings. Generally at this point, companies meet a new challenge of meeting demand, and often fall into problems in their ability to meet that demand. As customer awareness increases, the wants and needs of the consumer allow for competition to increase as new players enter the market. Over time in this phase, as competition increases, strategic pricing becomes necessary to maintain market share.

In the *Maturity Phase*, a focus on cost reductions is necessary, in order to maximize profitability and to provide ongoing strategic pricing in order to maintain market share. Sales volumes begin to peak, and market saturation becomes apparent. Due to the proliferation of competing products, prices tend to begin a decline. The company begins to focus on brand differentiation and feature diversification in an effort to maintain or increase the capping market share. Overall, the industrial profits as a unit begin to decline.

In the *Decline Phase*, costs become counter-optimal as sales volumes begin to decline. The business ingrains to cost-cutting scenarios to bleed out remaining dollars. Overall, prices and profitability begin to diminish. In keeping with the cost-cutting scenarios, profit objectives become a challenge of product / distribution efficiency rather than through increased sales.

The above is an example of more convention. Sure, there are numerous examples that can be sited to support this hypothesis; however, there are also other examples that have gone against the grain. There are people who have taken a dying product and reinvigorated it. There are leaders who have done the same in an industry. Just think about the airline industry and the introduction of low-cost carriers. These innovators were told that they were crazy to enter the market, and yet, they are now the leaders. Nothing is certain, no matter how hard we attempt to rationalize it, so be careful of the convention you choose to buy into.

We believe that one of the biggest reasons companies fail early on is they buy too far into convention, on a couple of fronts. As we have surveyed start-up companies, we asked them why they chose to get into business, and they have told us that they wanted to be their own boss and that they wanted more free time to spend with family. Generally these are common beliefs, a convention held by a majority of people who are working for others. You know, "The grass is always greener on the other side." perspective. Now, if you have been in business for any length of time, you will know that in running a business, there are many sleepless nights, and while you are your own boss, at times you are not.

The second convention that they buy into is, "I will provide it, and they will come." Many times, we have seen start-ups prepare a business and marketing plan that on the surface looks promising, go out and find a space, make a website, have business cards printed, and then find that it hasn't turned out the way they thought it would. Part of this convention is created early on, by well-meaning family and friends. Naturally they want to be supportive, so they tell the new entrepreneur what a wonderful idea he or she has and that they will support him or her. In the end, while the idea may have been promising, when the rubber hits the road, he hasn't built the thinking that ultimately generates the success. He gets locked up in belief, and when things don't work out the way she planned, she is unable to recover.

At any given point of time, know there is a prevalent thinking at play in your environment. This, in and of itself, is neither good nor bad. There is certainly convention that works. If there weren't a convention in place that had us believe that when we took a check to the bank, we would see the funds in our account, then that would add an entirely different level of complexity to running a business. However, at the same time, there is convention that doesn't work, and in fact, locks you up to possibility. The challenge as a leader is to be able to identify the convention at play on either side and to act contrarily when need be to take advantage of the opportunities. If you look at some of the greatest - Warren Buffet, Steve Jobs, Richard Branson - can you see how that thinking has worked for them?

If we look at nature, we can see that there are natural cycles at play. In fact, they act almost as a pendulum. There is a sway back and forth to everything, and this natural swing helps to balance and regulate our world. In order to believe something, you need to not believe another, but in order to know the other, you need to have experienced it. In business, if we hadn't known the challenge of creating a product or service, we wouldn't know what growth was. In the stock market, if we hadn't experienced the down, we wouldn't know the up. There is a natural momentum to all things in the world - everything.

This natural momentum is oftentimes what convention is built from. These same tides are used to innovate and reinvent kingdoms, governments, and companies, and at the same time, can easily destroy them. We like to have certainty in what creates the ups and downs, so there are times when you are quick to buy into a reason as soon as it is linked with something that you believe to be true in that moment. There are many natural cycles at play at a micro and macro level when it comes to business. These are the parts of what makes running a business a challenge, and at the same time so much fun. As you start to recognize their swing and are able to circumvent the full sway to the other side, it allows you to generate new and creative ideas, and then to put those into practice, awaiting the next new challenge. This book is intended to challenge your thinking and to have you notice how some of the conventions of business, by your adopting them, can in fact make them become self-fulfilling prophecies, either good or bad. We tell our clients, based on this point, to choose wisely what they believe.

Have you ever noticed in our society, that "everybody knows"? You will even hear statements that we preface with the statement itself. "Everybody knows" that people are the number one asset of business. Well, if this is true, why are there so many issues with people in and around business? Really, who specifically said this? If we all really believed this at our core, how could people in fact be a problem in business? Our guess is that we don't all really believe it; we have just become comfortable in saying it, because that is what we should say, isn't it? This is the herd mentality at play again. How many times have you heard business phrases that over a period of time become the "buzz" words that everyone talks about? Are you caught up in the "buzz," or are you thinking differently?

What does the simple statement of "people are the number one asset of business" mean for you? If you were to ask your employees, would they have the same answers? There are certainly businesses and companies that believe this at the core and demonstrate it, each and every day. Then there are those who look at that company's success and adopt what they believe to be their thinking, hoping that by doing so, they will have the same. They are following the leader of the herd; however, just remember when you are following, it is only the leader who has the thinking about where you all are going. Everyone else is just focused on the hooves in front of them.

In 2001, everybody in the Canadian manufacturing industry knew things were good, and capacity to meet demand was the problem they were facing. Everybody at that conference knew that. That is, except for that one guy who called for a par Canadian dollar with the United States. Look around the world. There is so much "everyone knows" because, after all, it is just the way it is. What we will tell you is if you choose to buy in, you simply might as well go to sleep. If the herd makes up, say, 90 percent of the world and they all think the same conventions, do you think they innovate differently, or do they just spin old ideas differently, the same thought the next guy also thought? If you follow the herd, you miss the opportunities, and you get caught in the conventional problems associated with the thinking. What would happen if, for a moment, you began to question the world? What if what you were told was not real? What could you possibly create? What if you chose to believe the opposite? We know that, just in reading this, your mind is spinning with how many times you have heard "everybody knows," and now you are questioning that thinking. Good for you. You are on the path.

As we stated earlier, we believe that companies are a representation of the thinking and focus of the leader(s). You may agree or you may not; it is up to you. We often run into business leaders who look out at the world and their business and point fingers. We are great proponents of growing your thinking, as I am sure you are. Just for fun, grab a piece of paper and write down in your own words what "growing your thinking" means to you, right now. We predict that by the end of reading this book, you will find how your own thinking around this statement will have changed. However, the only chance that you will get to see this in action is if you choose to write it down now. Take the challenge.

So, let us ask you a question. How do you see the world of business and how it works? We mean, what are *your* rules for business and how it operates? Have you ever thought about that? Perhaps as you think of it, business is simply a list of all the beliefs that you have adopted from your mentors and peers, read about, heard about, or learned about while operating in your business. At any rate, all the things you know about business, have you ever really thought about where they came from?

Now for a moment, think of anything you learned in school. When you think about the rules of mathematics, English, or grammar, did you experience those firsthand and develop them yourself, or did you just adopt those rules to be true and not give them a second thought? How about when you think about business? Is what you believe truly yours? Are they your own original thoughts? Chances are no. How much is what you have experienced firsthand, and how much of it have you adopted from others? Now, are some of those beliefs real? Are they real for everybody? Did Steve Jobs, Bill Gates, Henry Ford, or Donald Trump believe the same rules as everybody else, or would their rules be different? Seems their results are different, so perhaps their rules are different.

Up to now, we have just recapped the ideas of what business is, and the rules we all generally follow. Those rules make up the convention, and may or may not be designed for your success. The dictionary meaning of *convention* and *business,* for those in disbelief, may surprise you.

Con-ven-tion, [Kuhn-**ven**-shuhn], noun
- a meeting or formal assembly, as of representatives or delegates, for discussion of and action on particular matters of common concern.
- an agreement, compact, or contract.
- an international agreement, especially one dealing with a specific matter, as postal service or copyright.
- a rule, method, or practice established by usage; custom: *the convention of showing north at the top of a map.*

Busi-ness, [**biz**-nis], noun
- an occupation, profession, or trade: *His business is poultry farming.*
- the purchase and sale of goods in an attempt to make a profit.
- a person, partnership, or corporation engaged in commerce, manufacturing, or a service; profit-seeking enterprise or concern.

"The convention of business," when we combine these two definitions as one example, means "an agreement, compact or contract, rule or method for the purchase and sale of goods in an attempt to make a profit." For some, the convention of business is simply, "the agreement, compact or contract, rule or method to an occupation, profession, or trade."

We are so bold as to say that in business, as in life, there are rules that have been developed that, once we choose to believe, govern and limit you. We are aware that for some of you, that will seem preposterous, because you believe rules are important. You may believe that rules are not mean to limit you. In fact, they are, and in some cases, for good reason. Rules are necessary. They keep our societies safe. They ensure access to essential services. They keep the playing field level. They tell us how we should operate. Tongue in cheek, sometimes we wonder if the reasons are in fact real, or whether this is marketing at work. However, either way, they guide you and give you certainty. Essentially, some people believe that rules are intended to limit you to the intention of the game. We believe that it is approximately 10 percent of business leaders who truly understand and think openly about how the conventional rules of business limit them in their intention of the game. The rest never give it a second thought, and they simply fall asleep to the herd type of thinking.

Convention limits you when it becomes part of the excuse for why it is that you are not doing what you want to do. Too many times we hear business leaders say, "The bank won't let me" or "This is just the way it is done in my industry" or "Everyone knows that the only way you can accomplish that is by ..." They become a victim to the thinking, instead of opening up their thinking to another way. There is always another way, when you know that you really want something.

Again, we ask you, what is your convention in business? Are those rules working for you, or are they keeping you busy? Do you really believe the playing field is level? Are the rules of business convention for Apple, Google, Facebook, Monsanto, Shell, or Exxon different from yours? Perhaps they understand a different convention and thinking in business.

We have met and worked with thousands of people within business, who are all very busy. Busy in the "right way" to run a business. Busy in the "everybody knows." A while back, we worked with one such business owner, who was working seven days a week, eighteen hours per day, maintaining his business. He had fallen into the trap of implementing ever-more-complex business systems, upgrading training, and documenting every process imaginable. We had him recognize there had been a shift in his intention in growing his business based on the rules he adopted in his industry. We give him credit for believing what we said about his company having become a reflection of himself, and that it had lost its innovation and creativity. As he questioned, learned, and experienced his own truth around business, over eighteen months he reduced his hours in the business by more than 50 percent, retained his current management and support staff levels, and increased his revenues by more than 34 percent. In changing his thinking, he changed how he interpreted the rules of business, to ultimately create a different result.

Consider for a moment that maybe this busi-ness could be part of what creates the staggering statistics in business failure. After all, doesn't everybody know only one in ten businesses will succeed and become profitable, or even worse, that less than 4 percent of businesses will be still be running and profitable one decade after start-up? We believe in order for any convention to exist, there has to be something or someone who would benefit from having us believe it was true. Do you think successful companies begin with this fear? For what purpose, for example, would this business convention exist? Could it be that these beliefs are the ones the 10 percent would have the rest of business believe? Do you think they believe something different?

Recognize your personal business convention is merely the rules that you have adopted about the way you should conduct business and how you interact with your employees, markets, customers, and the world. Some of the most innovative companies draw top talent from around the world. They attract top investment. They interact with their customers in a different way. They position themselves to be different and to respond differently. How do they create that?

Take this a step further. What if the convention of business, as you see it today and as you think you know it, is in fact not real? What if understanding this changes how you see the rules, creating new levels of thinking, openness to opportunities currently unseen, and awareness of your intention. Is it possible there is a different way of looking at the business of business? Welcome to opening the thinking of the top 10 percent.

The Model — Part One

In the work we have done with companies, we believe that as a company grows and faces challenges and obstacles, there comes with it, different ways of interpreting the environment it is operating within. We said, as in nature, there are cycles that come into play. There is a pendulum at work. While there are those who may argue this is just a business cycle, in fact, we believe it is in the ability of the leader(s) to question that environment in a different way, which produces a different result in traversing the natural business cycle.

Our focus is and remains around the type of thinking that is present within a company during the various phases of business. As you become aware of the thinking traps, it will allow you to seek alternatives, instead of being caught in the inevitability of the cycles. At times, it can be difficult to see the forest for the trees; however, there are other clues around that if you choose to notice will tell you, that indeed you are in a forest. We want to provide you with a perspective on the clues.

In our work, we have placed the thinking into four different phases. We have labeled them in the illustration below to coincide with a general sense of the thinking that is present in each one.

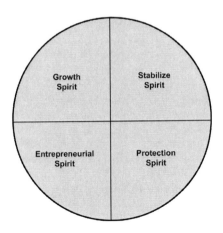

You will see that for illustration purposes, we have displayed these as if they were a cycle. All companies are transitioning through one, or even bridging two or more of these categories, depending on the prevalence of the thinking of the leader(s) and within the company at any given time. We do not believe that a leader or a company is solely contained in one phase of the cycle, and to have anyone believe this is the case would only concrete them even further into the perils of convention. We believe growth as a leader and as a company, in general terms, is always possible, though not necessarily guaranteed, and we present a different thinking in order to create something different for you and your organization. We fundamentally believe that real growth occurs in a business due to leadership that has a clear intention and a mind-set toward the outcome.

In the following chapters we will delve further into the thinking behind each of these phases, while exploring the impact of competing intentions and the resulting actions that are common in most companies as they experience each phase over time. Each phase plays an important role in the equation of growth or, alternatively, decline. We believe that when you, yourself, become aware of the micro and macro thinking at play, you will see alternatives for growth and abundance. When you look at business in general, if you take the time to notice the similarities, you will see there really is a cycle at play. This cycle is clear, and the patterns and actions that companies traditionally take in these cycles are predictable, as they enter or leave any one of the quadrants of the cycle. As we work through to define each of the phases, we will introduce the conscious and unconscious aspects of what is occurring. We will discuss the thinking of the leader and the organization and discuss the actions that generally result from the thinking in each phase.

Part of the fun in this will be that as you read through these chapters, you will gain an understanding of where you and your organization sit today. Remember, this is not a book of formula or recipe. You will have read those types of books; maybe they fit for you and maybe they don't. This book is intended to have you think, and for you to reacquaint yourself with the skills, resources, and thinking that make you the leader you know that you are. Some of you will read this and understand clearly and admit openly where you are, and take action to move your company in a different direction. That is what we want you to do. Others will want to reject some of the notions, saying, "I am different and this will not happen in my company." As you will learn, if you fight the cycles, you will fall victim to them. If you embrace them and use them, you will create something entirely different. We encourage you to be open. Be honest with yourself. As they say, once you admit it, you can change it. Many think there is comfort in being asleep, but when you are the one driving the bus, only you know when you need a pit stop. As we stated earlier, growth is possible, though not guaranteed.

To give you an example, early in our business, we had the opportunity to work with a medium-sized manufacturing company. The CEO, by all accounts, was a very smart businessman. He had an MBA, and he knew business and all the convention that went with it. He was well aware of business and product cycles and could easily quote what needed to be done in order to run his business. Admittedly, he had a strong personality, which had served him well, as he had done amazingly well in holding his intention in the face of many doubters who told him that the product offering he had would never sell. We give him full credit, for early on, the drive and passion of a new entrepreneur allowed him to build a market and he created success, very nearly overnight.

At the time we were introduced to him, he had found that his company's financial indicators were showing signs of strain, even though his sales were healthy, and upon the advice of a close friend called us for our thoughts. We screen our clients, so as part of this quick review of his company, we identified that the company's thinking was leaning more toward the stabilize and protection spirits. Process control, cost cutting, and squeezing of efficiency were his focus as the CEO. He was offering a great product. His company was still the market leader, although the industry, itself, was in decline. His focus shifted from servicing a market need, inward, to the challenges of the company, and he had lost all sight of the customer's future needs. After our review, we had a discussion on our observations and discussed how we believed that the thinking in the organization needed to be redirected. He scoffed, and told us how he was aware of what was happening and that the direction he had set for the organization was the proper one.

One of the premises we work under, as you will see, is that if you don't think you have a problem, then you don't. We absolutely respect there are people who see the world differently than we do, and that as a business leader or individual, you always need to do what you believe to be right. In fact, we appreciate that thinking, because that is the way we think. While

25

it was obvious to us that he needed to quickly evaluate his customers' needs to respond with new products and services, we also know it is easy to get "married" to something that has generated success for you. As we talked, he reiterated the story that many people had told him when he was going into the business—that he would never succeed—and how he had proved them wrong. He told us that he would prove us wrong as well. Less than nine months later, the company's doors closed, and in the end, he let his company die, in his need to be right.

The most successful business owners we have met are quick to take a calculated risk, and are equally as quick to change when something is not working. They have no need to be right personally, and in fact, they congratulate themselves for their flexibility. Admittedly, there are those times when they wish they had ended some venture sooner. However, they understand that how the market responds provides the feedback critical in each of the phases. They are honest and understand where they are. They understand and seek out where to find the right answers to get to where they want to go. More importantly, they believe that oftentimes, the answer is right in front of them; they just need to be open to it, and they will have found it.

When you look globally at the world of business, whether you are in China, Canada, Switzerland, Germany, or the United States, the cycle of business emerges. We know that there are four main phases to the cycle in terms of thinking, and they naturally will run over and over again, as long as the company remains viable. As you get the thinking behind each of the phases, you will start to question your own thinking, and you will see the success that being challenged brings. Ask the 10 percent who do this each and every day.

At this point, we need to introduce a premise that will become important later on as you start to think differently from the convention. Not apparently obvious to the broader population, human nature has a fundamental need for certainty. People strive for certainty, to know what they know. It is an unconscious drive and need; most often, people are unaware of it. For those who have studied Carl Graves and his theory of evolution of humans through the values systems, you will already be aware of this. The need for certainty relates to a significant portion of the work you do as leaders inside your organization. While we will discuss certainty and uncertainty in greater detail in a later chapter, for now, all you need to know is that it is one of the underlying principles of how you operate as a human being. Naturally, we are all seeking to find certainty, although we generally don't realize that it is uncertainty that gives us movement. When we are uncertain, we are open to discover, to contemplate, to consider, and to learn as we evaluate the world around us, although there is generally little outward action or movement. We are building certainty in our minds. At the point you become certain in your mind, there is a burst of outward energy, which is focused around creating a physical world to match that certainty in your mind. When those two things match, you lose momentum, until the uncertainty once again creeps into our thinking and we start the process again.

It is at those points when the physical and mental match that we become bored and either consciously or unconsciously create uncertainty in order to allow us to create the motivation to move once again. For example, if you were certain you knew everything about business performance, then there is no way you would be reading this book. At some point, just before you picked it up, you let uncertainty creep in, and that allowed you to open up to a different way of thinking, which is what continues to motivate you to read on. If in the first chapter, you were certain that this was the same old thing, then you wouldn't be here right now. Some people create all kinds of uncertainty, all the time, and never move out of their minds. You know who we mean. Others can get caught on the other side, where everything is certain all the time. It doesn't matter where you are; the other is available to you. We tell our clients that from confusion always comes clarity, and this is this principle at play. You can't create growth in the physical plane unless you work through the uncertainty in your mind and become certain of what you want.

We bring up this point here, because it is important to understand, at a high level, in order to transition through the phases of the model, this principle is at play in the thinking. In each of the phases, there are areas of certainty and areas of uncertainty. It is the motivation that is created in moving from one side of the pendulum to the other that propels you into the next phase. The transition through the quadrants contains these shifts, as the uncertainty from a previous quadrant drives the need for certainty in the next, and so on through the cycle. This motivation, generally speaking, is unconscious to the leader and inside the organization, however it creates the bias for action in any given phase, and this is where you must shift your attention in order to get ahead of the curve. As you read the following descriptions of the phases, be aware and think about where your own bias for action is. Notice the behaviors that result from that thinking. Ask yourself, "What things am I seeking to gain certainty on, and as such, what uncertainty will fall out by taking the action I am choosing to take?"

Entrepreneurial Spirit

In the first quadrant of business, there is an *Entrepreneurial Spirit.* This is an exciting time. The bias for action in this stage is challenge, and the challenge of launching the business or new product / service is taken on tirelessly. The business owner or leader has a product or service to offer, she understands that to be successful she must have a product / service in want or need by a market, and she works incredibly hard to establish this market. For the first-time business owner, there is much to learn in regard to effective marketing, sales strategies, creating / manufacturing the product / service, learning the intricacies of running a business, budgets, finance, and in many cases the value of money, return on investment, and cash flow. Failure to execute in any of these can often be the difference between making it through or failing.

In this phase, the leader will leverage his networks and other non-competitive resources to assist him in developing the new thinking that is required in creating a viable business / product / service. If those resources are available within the company, then the leader actively engages "a team" and encourages them to expand their creativity and innovation, in order to pursue multiple options, knowing that some will be viable and others will lead to other ideas. As a leader, he is in constant refresh and learning mode in terms of his skills, knowledge, and expanding capabilities. He is constantly challenging himself to expand his thinking into new areas and is willing to do whatever it takes to keep his thinking fresh.

The leader or company in this quadrant will generally have high energy and enthusiasm, and at times it can appear that she is driven by blind ambition. This blind ambition and the drive behind it can, for many, be effective as she navigates seemingly unaware of the pitfalls surrounding her at times. She just pushes through even what on the surface can be seen as impossible obstacles. Many seasoned entrepreneurs who begin with this blind ambition reflect on this stage later, in shock and amazement that they made it.

In this phase, the leader is amazingly customer centric. He is finely tuned to the needs and wants of the customer. He intimately gets to know his customers, which for many, allows further innovation and enhancement of his products. At the end of the day, he knows success in the company is about meeting the customer's needs, and he will do what it takes to do so. The customer is therefore the focus.

The leader fundamentally understands that the answer in terms of innovation and creativity does not mean throwing money at the problem, and in fact, some of the best ideas have come from having nothing. In terms of spending, the new entrepreneur, generally through need, is extremely frugal. She is aware of the dollars going out and the dollars coming in, and begins to learn the intricacies of the cash flow game. The leader who learns that cash is king, and the importance of return on investment in everything about her business, will yield well over time. At this stage, the focus of investment is on the product / service and on expanding the thinking of the group.

In this phase, there is a willingness to do what it takes. The business leader and team will be very sacrificial in terms of their own time and needs. They will take on many roles, and will do many different things inside the company. This is a great learning stage for everyone involved, including the leader, and generally as they come through this stage, they have an amazing knowledge of the product / service, customer, and operations. Individuals chosen to be part of the team are selectively recruited for their skills and knowledge set and are expected to demonstrate their flexibility in many areas. At this stage, the team operates openly, and as a result, everyone knows everything. The team is dynamic, and they are inspired to work tirelessly in order to launch the new product / service or company and have it be successful.

Cash generally remains tight throughout this entire phase. Initial costs of investment can be high, and sales low relative to those initial costs. Sales steadily increase throughout this phase; however, time passes before the profitability curve begins to emerge. The response and sales within this phase lend to giving certainty to the market / product / service and business, and confidence translates into the motivation around the uncertainty of capturing more market, thus propelling them into the next phase.

For the mature company, which reenters this phase, cash may be more readily available based on its previous success and growth. This said, a mature business leader is aware of the return on investment and cash game and understands that throwing money at a problem is not innovation. He pushes to create new products / services, and through focusing on innovation and creativity, he understands that he will set the tone for product / service profits throughout the company's life cycle. Even for proven companies, this requires significant balance. It can be easy to get "married" to a concept or idea, and fail to see the forest for the trees; it generally falls on the business leader to beware of "the die to be right scenario." Bill Gates is quoted as saying, "Success is a lousy teacher. It seduces smart people into thinking they can't lose."

This phase is filled with the seeds of success, and at the same time, the tears of failure. If the company, team, and leader are able to navigate the perils of this phase, they will ultimately find their success. However, it often takes throwing up a hundred different ideas before one will stick. For the new entrepreneur, and even for some seasoned leaders, experiencing a failure in this phase can impact their ability to recover. They expend so much energy and resources in this phase that they ultimately let fear overtake them. It is the stories of Apple or Google that have anyone entering into this phase recognize that possibility does exist and they, too, could have the next greatest idea. We believe that there is no such thing as failure, and it is those leaders who interpret perceived failure simply as feedback, that are able to push through this phase.

In 1984, Fredrick W. Smith, the CEO of Federal Express, launched Zapmail. Federal Express had become a industry leader in the delivery world, and he felt this new addition would revolutionize the world of mail. The premise itself seemed brilliant. He already had a captive customer base in the hopper to leverage.

Zapmail was launched just prior to the rise in popularity of fax machines in business and in homes. The premise was that companies could expedite the sending of documents by "faxing" them from one Federal Express location to another. Federal Express would prepare paper copies of the documents and deliver them to the recipient within hours of the transmission. Smith believed that customers would pay a premium to have documents delivered within hours versus days, and by moving document travel from the existing trucks and aircrafts, new capacity would be opened within the company.

Federal Express proposed charging $35.00 per ten-page document. Simultaneous to the launch, the availability of fax machines gained prominence in business. Companies realized the cost efficiency and convenience of owning their own fax machines, and even when Fed Ex dropped the price to $10 per ten-page document, customers still scoffed at the idea.

Smith had underestimated the speed of adoption for this new technology into the marketplace. He ignored the issue of confidentiality and the requirement for quality documents. He failed to understand his customer's business, and in a short span of two years, Federal Express lost $350 million dollars in the Zapmail fiasco before they terminated the operation to refocus on their core business. Even brilliant business minds that have built massive companies can misread a market. Smith credits his willingness to abandon bad ideas and move on as key to growing to $39 billion dollars in revenue in 2011. He chose to interpret this as feedback, instead of failure.

Steve Jobs, perhaps one of the greatest innovators in the world, also had his moments. Take, for example, his little known venture NeXT, following his first departure from Apple. This product ended up completely missing the mark, never selling, and ultimately cost him and his investors hundreds of millions of dollars. Did this stop him, or did he use this as feedback, in order to recognize something else?

These stories highlight how difficult it can be to transition from the entrepreneurial spirit phase, on to the growth spirit. Even those who have built massive empires and success have had their share of misses. So what is the difference in this case of those who make it and those who do not?

Companies with great products that impact markets consistently leave you with a feeling, an experience, of something great, something different. Behind this, there is a leader and a team that hold an intention, create a laser focus on the outcome, and manage and understand the swing from uncertainty to certainty. They interpret the world slightly differently, and in doing so, impact the way in which we interpret it as well.

Growth Spirit

In the second quadrant of business is a *Growth Spirit*. This is, again, an exciting time. The leader and the team remain with high energy and excitement. They realize they haven't made it yet, though they are getting close enough to taste success. They have identified and continue to build their market as the order book starts to grow. At a point, they are required to seek additional resources and question their ability to meet demand.

The bias for action in this quadrant is toward "scramble." The team and leader refocus their efforts away from the product / service development, to building the delivery and supply chain systems to support the customer demand. The leader lets go of the need for new knowledge and skills development and is consumed in realizing his success. He becomes more logical and evaluative versus innovative and blind in his ambition as he taps into the knowledge base of the conventional practitioners of business. He becomes more and more aware of the pitfalls and potential issues around them as he engages and leverages additional staff and financial resources in order to meet customer demand.

In this phase, the entrepreneur is still customer centric; however she is now less focused on the product / service and more focused on how it will be delivered in a way to meet customer demands for service and quality. The focus shifts toward operations and setting up more formal internal systems. There is the dividing of jobs, and the idea of formal job descriptions comes into play. Some innovation continues; however, the focus is on the functionality of the product or service in its end application, although generally not at risk of slowing delivery of product. At the end of the day, she knows success for the company is about meeting customer demand, and she will do what it takes to do so.

In terms of spending, the revenue coming in, for the first time, is greater than the expenses going out, at least at the beginning of the phase. The company has become profitable, and in some cases, very profitable. The leader has become very execution centric, and is generally very quick to make decisions, including using cash to resolve issues. This is where a switch begins to occur. In the first quadrant, funds were tight and overcapacity to deliver product was available; now funds are available and capacity is tight. The scramble precipitates an "all hands on deck" mind-set, and suddenly family members and friends are often offered up as a solution for filling the labor needs of the organization. The focus on strategic critical skills for the organization is bypassed in the attempt to get the job done. There is the ability to buy the "nice to haves," and the struggle for control between those who were there from the start and the people who have been hired on can begin to surface. Entitlement issues start as well, which only feeds that struggle for control.

The business leader generally remains very sacrificial in this phase, at least initially; however, as mentioned above, he may begin to sacrifice cash in the meeting of customer demand. The addition of labor is generally large in comparison to the start-up numbers. Recruiting has shifted to "just get bodies that can do what we need," and as such, the underlying knowledge about the company, the product / service, and the customer is more centric to key individuals. While in the entrepreneurial spirit phase, everyone knew everything that was going on, however as the company grows in this phase, information sharing becomes more compartmentalized. The scope and breadth of job responsibilities per employee has been decreased, and focus is emerging on specific tasks. In many companies, as they move through this phase, the scramble can place increased pressure and stress on key employees as they wonder how long they can keep up this pace. More times than not, they believe that if they just had more resources, this would relieve the pressure, and yet the more resources they have, the more issues seemingly arise. The general lack of strategic recruiting and operational systems in this phase means that as resources are being added, they are not always effective. This creates an emotional spiral as finger-pointing begins to emerge, with the employees of the organization becoming more individually focused on what they want and need.

As the company moves through this phase, it will often experience the tightening of margins as a result of lower efficiencies. The ad hoc adding of resources to meet demand has eroded consistency and performance within the company. It is common to hear that the leader and key team members are tired and that they deserve to celebrate their success. Part of the tightening of margins will be as a result of large increases in compensation for these key people in the organization. This erosion of margins leads the company to the stabilize spirit quadrant, in which control becomes the driving force.

As a business leader, managing growth can be every bit as much a challenge as creating and developing a product / service for market. While the thinking in the first phase was about looking out at the possibility of the future, in this phase, the leader is confronted with the issues of the "here and now," which starts to bring the thinking more inward. The inward thinking pulls the leader away from her intention and focus, and when it does, can oftentimes be the downfall of a company; the seeds for failure are planted in this phase.

It is easy to see those companies that are in this phase. Accolade, Inc., is a built-for-purpose health services company that offers the employees and the families of large, self-funded employers a new employee benefit that simplifies the complexity of health benefits and the overall health system. Accolade delights employees, improves productivity, and cuts health benefits costs by 10 to 15 percent by helping health care consumers make better decisions and get the right care the first time.

Accolade continues to add to its portfolio of large employer customers, which is fueling its revenue growth and job expansion. Located in suburban Philadelphia, Accolade has recently expanded to a third office to support the over 200+ area jobs it has created in the last two years.[2]

This company is experiencing significant growth. Just this information alone can tell us what phase the company is experiencing. It is generating revenue and expanding at an incredible rate. Its success will hinge on its ability to remain focused on its intention and to drive this growth based on that focus.

Leaders and Innovation

In the first two phases, we are clear that there is a mind-set at play. The leaders are leading, and they are leading through innovation and passion. Please do not confuse this solely with "fad" products and ideas, because to do so would miss the point. It is more than that. These leaders have a different focus. They believe that anything is possible. They believe they can impact the industry or even the world. Ask yourself, how do you see what you are doing?

Innovative leaders consistently have opportunity in their sights. They do not get caught up in the perceived problems, and instead choose to focus on the opportunity. We have all heard about the need to be innovative, and at times, may even believe that you are; however, we daresay we have witnessed few with this mind-set. Again, the herd mentality is most often at play. As we will explore further, most are trained to think inside the problem and look for solutions to lead them out. The truth of the matter is that through holding an intention and focus of innovation, unconsciously a leader is in a mode of creation. He or she holds a different thinking. The question is never "Why is this happening?" but instead, "How do I resolve this?"

Take, for example, the dictionary meaning of *innovation*:

Innovation, [in-*uh*-**vey**-sh*uh*n], noun
- Something new or different introduced: *numerous innovations in the high school curriculum.*
- The act of innovating; introduction of new things or methods.

Unconsciously, in holding the idea and intention of innovation, the leader is in a mode of creation. He is in a constant mode of new ideas, things, and methods of building ideas, concepts, and products. Naturally, the premise of this thinking is expansive, and therefore it implies growth. The entire lefthand side of the model works in this vein. At the onset of a new product / service or business, the seeds of innovative thinking are in place, and over time, this thinking expands and grows to its full potential. Through this growth in thinking, growth in the environment occurs. This materializes as company growth, and as with all tides of growth, there are tides of consolidation or decline. Following the innovation cycle, the pendulum swings, and a new cycle emerges as the business leader takes his company into the third and fourth quadrants of stabilize spirit and, ultimately, protection spirit.

The Model – Part Two

Stabilize Spirit

In the third quadrant of business is a *Stabilize Spirit*. In this phase, the company has proven its ability to meet demand and to service a market; however, through the scramble of doing so, it has come to realize there are internal issues that need to be addressed. The quality and cost challenges from the previous quadrant have created instability in the company. Key members of the team, including the leader, are tired, and as a result, there can be a propensity to sell the company, or if you are an employee, to look at other alternatives. The leader realizes that the ad hoc manner of adding resources in the previous phase has created issues, and she seeks to resolve these.

The leader starts to shift his focus internally to the company and away from the influence of the customer. He reflects on what is perceived to be chaos, as he hears repeatedly about the challenges occurring within the company from key personnel. He recognizes and starts the path of building stability. He engages his team in establishing processes related to operations and quality, in an attempt to limit the impact of nonstrategic and underskilled labor. He focuses on reducing nonessential spending and forgoing leadership development for himself and his teams. He reduces spending in the areas of research and development, technology, human resources, and in some cases, sales, telling himself once he gets past this present hurdle, he will grow those areas again in a different way. The innovative and creative side of the company is being contained, in favor of logical, deductive methods of thinking. He builds full-on organizational charts and job descriptions in an attempt to refocus the organization on what is important.

In some cases, in this phase, a new business leader is brought in to run the company, in order to bring about the stability that is required. If the original leader remains in place, she begins to believe that the blind ambition she started with is now seemingly the monster that created the problems of today. For some companies, this is the start of external assistance to gain control, as they bring in consultants and experts to assist them in stabilizing their company.

The leader and team have shifted their focus almost solely inward in an effort to correct the confusion and scramble within the organization. In this phase, they may start to see a reduction in demand from the customer, although there will be a belief that it is just a minor blip and the salespeople will be continuing to forecast strong sales in the upcoming quarters. Technology integration within the company will be seen as a solution, and will be presented in a way to demonstrate a positive return on investment. Ideas such as statistical process control, lean, quality management, and box- or control-type thinking emerges as more and more controls are put into place.

As the company moves through the phase, company measurement systems and reporting begin to emerge. Management develops strategic plans and conducts numerous meetings around providing status on these. They measure and analyze everything. The company studies the competition and focuses on maintaining market share. In the early phases of the cycle, while the leader is aware of the competition, they build relationships with their customers and build certainty in addressing their needs. Now they start to focus and compare themselves and identify the weaknesses in the competitor's product and tell themselves about the superiority of their own products and services. They even implement different pricing strategies and giveaways in an attempt to differentiate themselves from their competition.

Initially within this phase, the profitability of the company increases, as a result of the control initiatives that have been put in place. However, we know this in itself can create problems. As customer demand begins to decline or there is a loss of market share to other competitors, the leader may fool himself and the team into thinking, "Well, that's okay, we are more profitable on a lower sales volume, so in the end we are doing better." This will hold true only as long as the demand remains flat or goes up, although generally this is rarely the case. The leader becomes more evaluative and logical in his decision making, and with the flood of data available to him, he becomes cautious about taking risk. The company is mature, and investors are depending on it to be solid.

The profitability of the company continues to strengthen throughout the beginning of this phase. However, as competitors continue to enter the market with new innovation, a different pressure begins to emerge. At this point, the company has two different directions that it can go. Depending on the strength of the company, it either reallocates resources or seeks investment in order to reallocate resources to drive back into the entrepreneurial spirit, or takes the unfortunate path of doing nothing, where it continues the cycle downward into the protection spirit.

Protection Spirit

The fourth quadrant is the *Protection Spirit*. At the beginning of this phase, the company is easily able to meet demand with contained processes and efficiency. There is a renewed stability in the company in this regard, although the market demand for the product has peaked and is in decline. This issue in and of itself prompts further cost reductions to hold acceptable margins as sales slowly decline. As the company continues to focus on the competitor for answers, it takes on almost a victim mentality. It begins to blame its supply chain for not being responsive in cost cutting and applies pressure in this area. It begins to blame its customers for switching to competitors and believes that there is more at play than what really meets the eye. The focus changes, to beating the competition on price, and in some cases, a strategy of deep undercuts is employed in an attempt to put the competition out of business. The company is so focused on beating the competition that it loses even further touch with the needs and wants of its customers and believes that it knows better what they really need.

In this phase, the business leader's bias for action is around cost cutting. With this focus in mind, the company continues cutting expenses not deemed to be essential to the operation. Consolidation occurs in nondirect product- or service-related departments, with unskilled and untrained labor being required to fulfill the duties and maintain processes that were defined in the previous phase. There is an increased pressure to continue to increase efficiency, with little acknowledgment that many of the systems and processes that were developed for control previously are not sized for use in this ever-shrinking environment. The processes and systems that were implemented begin to choke nonessential resources, and there is generally an exodus of labor as this takes place.

Throughout this cycle, pricing pressures continue, and as such, margin begins an erosion cycle. The company is now clearly in the decline stage of the product and business life cycle. Yet, unconsciously, the focus of the competitor stealing your customers and the need to cut costs dominates the landscape and the thinking. This is often the phase of "die to be right." The business leader has grown a company, often against the odds, and this will ingrain further in her thinking that somehow she has been wronged. However, she fails to realize what her focus on uncertainty is telling her and instead attributes the struggle to the actions of the competitor. The unconscious behavior to get certainty in costs and in order to stabilize profit drives the company deeper into cost-cutting scenarios. It becomes a vicious cycle. The cost cutting in response to price and market erosion becomes merely a stay-alive scenario.

At this point, company morale is in full decline. There are numerous closed-door meetings and there is little, if any, information being shared. Production and service efficiency begin to decline. Management and leadership become stagnant and tired, almost as if unconsciously they know they are fighting a lost cause. They become secretive in response to their focus on the competition, and they move into a self-protection mode. Employees recognize that they need to start looking out for themselves, as they have experienced multiple rounds of layoffs at this point, and so their focus moves beyond the company to new opportunities.

At the beginning of this phase, as discussed, margins may be stable, but at this point, cash flow becomes an issue for the company when its expenses begin to exceed its revenue. There is such a fight to hang on that any cash reserves or investment dollars are focused on continuing the operation. In this phase, there will be numerous ideas and concepts being thrown around, although the company will be so resource-constrained there will be little possibility to actualize them.

In most cases, the company will cease to exist, or it will get bought out by its competitor for pennies on the dollar. There are very rare cases when a company has recovered from being full-on in this phase, and in those instances, they have generally been taken over by someone who views the company as a start-up.

Case Examples

Of course, in the work we do, we are always curious about what companies are doing, where the thinking of their leader is, and how they are operating in this changing environment. There are some companies we find interesting, not because they are good or bad companies. In fact, we don't believe a company is either. They are sometimes a little like children: "they are only going through a phase." As you will see in later chapters, there is never one right answer when it comes to moving a company through a phase; there is only the ability to change the thinking.

We want you to be clear about how easy it can be to see what we are talking about, so let's take a look at two different companies, Research in Motion and Crocs. They have very different stories, and you will notice how different the thinking is in each.

In 2008, Research in Motion Limited was a massive success story, and even as concerns about the economy were surfacing, analysts believed it was going to continue to buck the trend. Due to its innovation around its handsets and in the security of its platform, Research in Motion was positioned to be the ideal business solution worldwide and its business was taking off.

The graph below outlines the revenue, operating income, and margins over the past four years, and provides us with a perspective on what has taken place in the company.

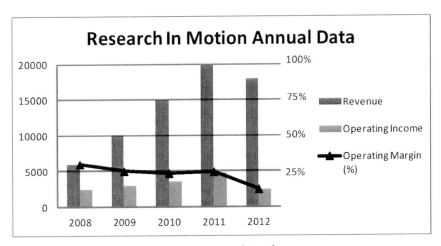

RIMM Annual Data[3]

Please note that the 2012 number is a projection, based on Q1 actual and forecasted revenues. The chart below breaks down 2011 and the first quarter of 2012, and we get a closer look at the company as a whole.

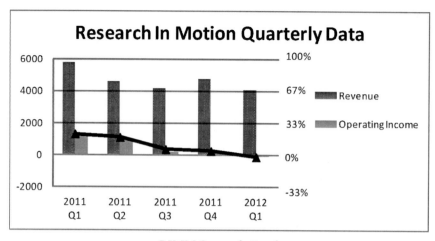

RIMM Quarterly Data[4]

As you can see, through 2011, it experienced operating margin pressure. This same trend holds true quarter over quarter. The company, based on the data, appears to be experiencing either a decline in market share or a decline in pricing power due to competition or both. Sales revenue is unstable or flattening over the previous five quarters, with a slight decline. In the annual chart, the revenue for 2012 is expected to decline for the first time.

This information provides one clue in determining which phase the company is predominantly operating in; however, in order to further understand, you need to assess the thinking of the leader(s). Here is a second clue. The following are excerpts from a Marketwire release on May 29, 2012, from the company's CEO.

> In terms of challenges, as I mentioned on the March financial results conference call, RIM is going through a significant transformation as we move towards the BlackBerry 10 launch, and our financial performance will continue to be challenging for the next few quarters. The on-going competitive environment is impacting our business in the form of lower volumes and highly competitive pricing dynamics in the marketplace, and we expect our Q1 results to reflect this, and likely result in an operating loss for the quarter. We are continuing to be aggressive as we compete for our customers'

business—both enterprise and consumer—around the world, and our teams are working hard to provide cost-competitive, feature-rich solutions to our global customer base ...

We continue to make strategic changes to RIM's senior management team with the hiring of two key new members to RIM's executive leadership team. Kristian Tear, our Chief Operating Officer, whose background also includes extensive experience in international sales in Europe, Asia and Latin America, and Frank Boulben, our Chief Marketing Officer, who will provide our team with deep experience in the mobile computing and communications industry. Both will assist me and the existing executive team as we continue to make the organizational changes necessary to position RIM for the future and prepare for the launch of our new BlackBerry 10 platform ...

The CORE (cost optimization and resource efficiency) program we told you about previously is focused on delivering key operational savings through various initiatives. The financial objectives for the CORE program are targeted to drive $1 billion in savings by the end of fiscal 2013, based on our Q4 run rate. We are targeting better efficiency and use of resources in our sales and marketing initiatives to effectively leverage marketing windows and evaluate our country portfolio to determine where it makes sense for us to prioritize our efforts. We will also continue to review RIM's organizational structure and clearly define accountabilities for all key businesses and business processes with a goal of eliminating fragmentation, duplication and inefficiencies. While there will be significant spending reductions and headcount reductions in some areas throughout the remainder of the fiscal year, we will continue to spend and hire in key areas such as those associated with the launch of BlackBerry 10, and those tied to the growth of our application developer community. We will share more details regarding our progress throughout the year as programs are implemented or changes are completed. [5]

So, what do you think? Which phase do you predominantly see them operating from?

In reading the above news release, it becomes a little clearer where the company is. The communication, as you pay attention to and evaluate what is said, noting the quadrant similarities, confirms what we saw in the tables. There are key ideas, phrases, and words that also provide clues:

- Competitive environment impacting business in terms of lower volumes and competitive pricing.
- The company will see an operating loss for the quarter.
- Strategic changes in RIM's senior management team.
- The CORE program, or Cost Optimization and Resource Efficiency, focused on driving $1billion in savings by the end of fiscal 2013.

The CEO continues to look to the BlackBerry 10 as the savior of the company. In fact, at this point, he needs to, because the alternative is not all that attractive. If the company has truly reengaged innovation, then at this point, it could be straddling the entrepreneurial phase and the stabilize phase. If this were the first time that we had heard that the company was going to launch a revolutionary new product, then this could certainly be the case. The launch of the BlackBerry Playbook was supposed to be that; however, they were late to market, and the product did not impress, so it leaves some doubts at this point. More likely the company is in the stabilize phase, and depending on the success of its launch for the BlackBerry 10, could soon find itself staring down the protection phase.

No company, no matter how large or small, is immune to the cycles. Perhaps Bill Gates is correct when he says success can be your undoing. Is this the case for Research in Motion?

The second company that has an interesting story is Crocs. Its launch occurred in late 2002, at a boat show in Florida. The interest was so high in the product that the fire marshal was concerned over the blocked aisles that resulted. In that show, they sold a thousand pairs in three days.

That was the start of the craze; however, the idea and the company were formed over a weekend. Scott Seamans came across a strange clog developed by Fin Project NA, a Canadian company, for use primarily in day spas. Seamans saw the product as ideal for boating, and while on vacation in the Caribbean, showed the shoe to Lyndon Hanson and George Boedecker. Over the weekend, the Crocs Company emerged. Boedecker took charge of designing the first Crocs shoes, and acted as CEO from the inception in 2002. This weekend in 2002 represented the vision of what the Crocs Company would ultimately become.

Boedecker brought with him a wealth of business experience, having owned over a hundred Dominos Pizza franchises prior to moving to Quiznos in 1996, where he owned and operated several franchises throughout Oregon and Washington states. Also during this time, he worked directly for Quiznos Corporation in Canada as the executive vice president and chief operating officer of international sales and operations.

Following that show in late 2002, the company, recognizing the demand for its product, went to work to build in the innovation that would translate the company into a lasting entity rather than the overnight fad so typical in the fashion world. Comfort and function have always been in the forefront for the Crocs Company. In the early days, the product was focused on boaters and gardeners. The nonslip sole, featherlight weight of the clunky shoe, and amazing feel had the market's attention in a big way. Add to this the material the Crocs are made of, known as Croslite, a soft, bacteria-resistant material that fit the needs of the customer in diverse applications. It didn't take long for nurses, doctors, and the like to catch on to the benefits of the product.

So, how did they do it? The group knew they were on to something almost immediately, and while they positioned themselves to take advantage of the growth through warehousing and manufacturing, their focus remained on innovation and further application for their product. They applied that innovative thinking to their supply chain. By mid 2003, the company had purchased additional molds from Italy and opened another manufacturing warehouse in Colorado. By the end of that year, it had more than doubled production and added inventory management solutions. Revenues exceeded 1.2 million in that fiscal year. In 2004, Ron Snyder became an important member of Crocs, and he believed that Crocs could continue the growth trend if it could reduce the turnaround time for ordering and reduce the total order quantities for retailers. Crocs did this by purchasing Fin Project NA, the Croslite compound manufacturer, and creating a vertically integrated system. With this purchase, the company owned the resin manufacturing, shoe manufacturing, and distribution of the entire product line.[6]

In 2005, the company began preparing to go public, and officially changed its name from Western Brands to Crocs. In the same year, the company launched its first national advertising campaign, being recognized as "Brand of the Year" by *Footwear News*. With over five thousand retailers on board, the company sold six million pairs of shoes for $109 million in revenues and a first-time profit of $16.9 million. In 2006, the company went public (CROX); early guidance of $13 to $15 per share was low, as on February 8, 2006, the IPO sold 9.9 million shares at $21. The result was the largest IPO in history for a shoe manufacturer.[7]

Between 2004 and 2008, the company made a number of acquisitions:

- Crocs Canada (FKA Foam Creations Inc.) — a developer and manufacturer of products using resin-based Croslite material.
- Jibbitz, LLC — a manufacturer of charms stylized the Croc Shoes.
- EXO Italia — a developer and designer of ethylene vinyl acetate products for the footwear industry.
- Ocean Minded Inc. — a designer and manufacturer of sandals for the beach and action sports.
- Tidal Trade Inc. — a distributor in South Africa.

In 2008, as financial markets melted down, the company took a severe hit. In the first quarter, revenue growth slowed, and the company experienced a loss of $4.5 million. The year continued in this fashion, and losses mounted to $185.1 million for the year. The vertical integration of the company's production facilities required the company to hold large inventories in each area, and as demand slowed, the company felt the effects of its cash being tied up in inventory. In response to this, the company began significant cost cutting, closing plants in Canada and Brazil and reducing manufacturing in Mexico and China.

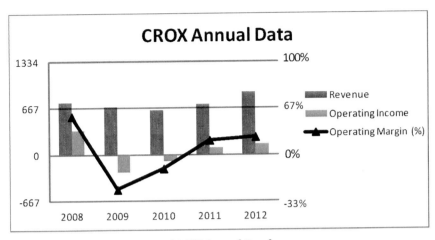

CROX Annual Data[8]

As can be seen above, the company created new growth after 2008. It continued the innovation and integration of new products into the line of offerings, as well as increased access to the Crocs brand around the world. It continued to invest in developing molds and shoe designs, and now presents a significantly different-looking shoe to the consumer, with the same comfort and functionality of the original Crocs. It has worked on the industry, specific to the products it offered, through acquisition and management of the supply chain. In its management of the supply chain, it has changed the face of how retailers forecast their needs, making all parties more profitable as a result. In its model, order timelines are significantly decreased, decreasing risk to the retailers and increasing flexibility in its product availability. In 2011, for the first time, the company exceeded $1 billion in annual revenue.

So, how about this company? Can you see how it moved through the cycle and where it used excess funds, from the stabilize phase, to reinvent itself? Can you see how it applied innovation to not just its products, but to its supply chain and other business processes? Do you notice how diligently it focused on its customer?

Crocs is a company that has found a way through the quadrant of protective spirit through the planning that occurred long before the company was in the quadrant. Seeds that were planted earlier in the company began to take root through the company's decline, which allowed it to hold an intention in recreating itself.

Leaders and Control

In the third and fourth quadrants, there is a different type of thinking at play. In the first two quadrants, the thinking is of innovation, creativity, and remaining fluid with solutions in order to capitalize on opportunity. There is no doubt about it that this very thinking brings with it a host of challenges for a leader and a company, but there is an incredible amount of energy and excitement that comes with it, at least initially. At the point where everyone gets tired, the pendulum swings the other way, and the focus becomes about gaining control. The leaders start to focus on controlling the chaos, and they lead with control and structure as a mindset. When we say this, please do not confuse this with the tyrant leader. These leaders have a focus on fixing problems and getting the entire picture of the organization under control. These leaders can even be the ones who speak of empowerment. They speak of empowering others to take action in the intention of creating controls in the organization, however in this, they create the structure that in fact holds people back. At times they will themselves be frustrated, and if at their core, they are entrepreneurs, they will find this type of leading boring and unfulfilling.

Leaders in these quadrants consistently see more and more problems in their sights. They are flooded with data, with measures, and with functional staff arguing about where the focus for the organization needs to be. While opportunities may be presented to them, they see the need to fix this one last thing before they can possibly take advantage of the opportunity. The opportunity passes, and they are still busy fixing the next thing, because after all, you know there is always one last thing. At other times, literally, an opportunity immediately in front of them is unseen, as a result of the contractive and protective thinking that is in place. While as leaders you are trained to be problem solvers, to think your way out of the problem by finding a solution to lead you out. We know that the solution is never within the problem; when that is your focus, it can be hard to find solutions.

Take, for example, the dictionary meaning of control:

Control, [*khun*-**trohl**], verb, controlled, controlling
- to exercise restraint or direction over; dominate; command.
- to hold in check; curb: *to control a horse; to control one's emotions.*
- to test or verify (a scientific experiment) by a parallel experiment or other standard of comparison.

- to eliminate or prevent the flourishing or spread of: *to control a forest fire.*
- *Obsolete.* to check or regulate (transactions), originally by means of a duplicate register.

Unconsciously, the leader, in holding the idea of control, is in a mode of restraint or destruction. We know that on the surface, this is not the plan; however, these stages are the natural evolution of decline, or death, in order to create new again, in a different cycle. As stated, even in the dictionary meaning, control is to eliminate or prevent the flourishing or spread of. We understand that at this point, the leader is working through issues as perceived in the business, and for him the focus is on preventing or eliminating these issues. However, understand that the intention, in and of itself, propagates decline in all manner of speaking. Naturally, the premise of this thinking therefore is contractive, and therefore it implies death.

The entire righthand side of the model works in this vein. At the onset of the model cycle, growth occurs, but as a leader or company follows the cycle, protectionism emerges, as the decline or death cycle continues. Remember the world works in cycles, tides, and ebbs and flows. These are normal, natural cycles, and as part of this, so too does the business cycle run. Most often in business, we are taught the logical ways of thinking that tell us how to do things. Again, we will ask you, for those who create great business success, do they understand something differently? Do they understand the cycles? Do they understand how these tides work, and how they can use them to propel them in further growth?

Please understand that while a cycle is inevitable, we believe when you build an understanding of how you're thinking affects where you are, there is the possibility you can pull yourself and your company out of the cycle of decline and into a different cycle of growth. It is such business leaders who make up the 10 percent. Remember that growth as a leader, in general terms, is possible but is not guaranteed. Growth occurs in business that is of leadership clear of intention and with a mind-set toward an outcome. Stagnation occurs in a business that is of leadership with unclear intention and with a limited mind-set toward the outcome.

In the next chapter, we will discuss the micro and macro swings that are at play in the cycle. These come from a quantum view, and we promise those who pay attention will yield new ways of thinking about their environment. These new ways of thinking allow them to become expansive, even in cycles of decline. They allow them to polarize and hold intentions, as they understand truly where they are and what is unconsciously and naturally unfolding in front of them. They understand the unreal nature of events and opportunities.

The Pendulum Swing

We have discussed the conventions of business so far, and even the convention inside the natural cycle of business, through the four quadrants. Pay attention: these four quadrants are the norm and are certainly a convention in and of themselves. However, for those who know, polarizing your organization is possible so you can move beyond the contractive quadrants relatively easily and create a new cycle of growth. In this, you must however realize, you are in a cycle, and no amount of logical, conventional business thinking will alleviate this. In fact, it is thinking that somehow you can avoid this, that ingrains you even further into the inevitability of the cycle.

If you look to nature, we are constantly in a cycle of life and death, and this same thing applies to business. You cannot build a new belief unless you let go of an old one. You would not be leading a business unless you decided at some point to let go of being an employee. In order for something new to be created, you need to let go of an old way of thinking. This is natural, and while there are many who will attempt to fight the cycles, when you let go of anything, it allows you to seek something new and exciting.

We are sure you have seen or experienced examples of where people hung on to something too long. In fact, it can be a lot of work hanging onto things, especially when somewhere in your gut, you know you really need to let it go. How many times have you heard people say something like, "They are just resistant to change." In fact, we all are, even those of you who like a good change. You see, we all like to change when we become certain, but when you are uncertain, if you are honest, you don't like change. You certainly don't like it when change is being done to you. You will fight and sometimes die to be right, rather than open up to something new.

Just for a moment, think about the number of people who attempt to fight the inevitability of the cycles. In fact, there have been huge businesses and industries that have been created to support the masses' desire to avoid the cycles. The cosmetic surgery industry has been created to fight the cycle of aging. The vitamin and pharmaceutical industries have been created to fight the cycle of illness. This is big business, when you think about it.

We imagine by now, you are wondering, "Well, if this is all inevitable, then what is the alternative if there is one?" We know the answer is yes, there is an alternative; however, it is not in fighting the cycles, but in using the cycles. So, what does this mean? By the mere fact that you are reading this book, seeds are planted. You now know things you previously did not. You cannot un-know something once you know it, and this creates the curiosity to learn and grow. You are already on the path, as you choose to keep going forward. In other words, something has to die in order to generate life for something else. When the leader of a company recognizes this seemingly simple concept, she becomes the orchestrator. In the later chapters, we will discuss the thinking behind doing this, but for now, let's talk about what moves a leader and a business from one phase to the next in the cycle, or from one cycle into the next.

In a company, at a macro level, there exists a swing from expansive thinking to contractive thinking. In the first two phases, the thinking is focused on expansion, while the last two are focused more around contraction. Now this does not mean that a company solely sits on one side or the other. As we have discussed, there can be actions taking place that appear to counteract the other thinking in any given moment; however, the question is, where is the predominant thinking of the company? Just as we demonstrated in the case of RIM, they were preparing to launch a new product (expansive thinking), at the same time they were working diligently to cost cut and restructure (contractive thinking). As we said earlier, if the new product launch is innovative and fresh, this would in fact be expansive; however, if it is more geared at trying to keep up with the competitors, then even though it appears expansive, it in fact would fall into the contractive camp.

The thinking behind each of the phases is outlined below in the diagram. On the left, the leader enters into the entrepreneurial spirit quadrant with the early stages of spontaneity and innovation, and further ingrains to fully know those traits through the growth spirit phase, employing expansive thinking to do so. Upon knowing those, there is a level of uncertainty that enters that has him enter protective and fearful type thinking, running him into the stabilize spirit and protection spirit phases, driven through contractive thinking. The macro swing represents a shift in the larger picture of the two sides of the pendulum, expansion or contraction. It is the larger pendulum swings that change the focus and the thinking of the company and by association its results.

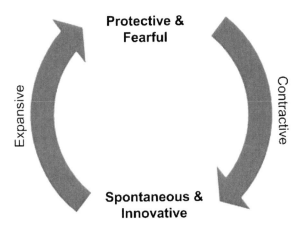

In the early stages, a leader creates a world around her that is passionate and excited. It is a world driven to succeed, committed to push through the barriers that come into play. Recognize, these barriers really only represent milestones. They represent movement, direction, and accomplishment. We tell our clients that, if they have no obstacles, then they have no intention, goals, or outcomes for the future. All business leaders have goals; however, the question is, "How do you perceive them?" Are they the walls that hold you back, or are they the bridge that spans the gap to the other side? Early-stage expansive thinking in the business cycle creates a landscape of bridges.

Also here, innovation and focus on the customer have business leaders focused outward on the world. In their effort to create something to serve a greater good, they are sacrificial of their own needs. You ever heard the saying, "You get what you give"? This is true for a business leader. In the perceived sacrifice of self, he actually creates expansion of self. We say "perceived" sacrifice of self because this is merely a perception depending on where you are in the equation. Many great leaders do not see it as self-sacrifice, and instead, see this as excitement and growth.

Expansive business leaders are passionate about their product and about servicing the world. They have customers who rave about their quality of service. They have a drive to reach more people and help them. They are genuine and passionate about the experience. They go above and beyond, and always focus on the result of enthusiastic customers. By the way, this does not mean customer satisfaction. There is a difference. Think of a time when you were satisfied. Did you want more of what satisfied you, or were you just satisfied and done? Customer satisfaction is a status quo business. True entrepreneurs engage their customers, leaving them with a state of being that has them enthusiastic about the product and service and telling everyone about it. Engaged and empowered customers are left with a feeling of wanting more. Customer loyalty is business loyalty to your customers. You get what you give.

The expansive business owner is thinking in terms of generating sales. She knows that product or service sales are what drive her growth. Touching a broader group, and being committed to your customers creates sales by creating a market to sell to. In the first two quadrants, the business owner has a focus on sales and generating revenue. In fact, she has to in order to stay viable.

In the first quadrant, the focus of the leader is on frugality. Now, you might think that this appears as a contractive intention. For a moment, think about frugality as key to innovation. Think about you, yourself, and where you became innovative in your own thinking when there were few resources available to tackle an issue. In the need to be frugal, the owner has a heightened awareness of new and different strategies and ideas to create and fill the needs of the business. In this, he actually holds the intention of creation of money, which is expansive thinking in its nature. In business convention, we hear a lack of money can be a hindrance to growth, whereas we see the same as true on the opposite side of the equation. In our experience, having excess money can stifle creativity and innovative thinking in the early stages, and in fact cripple the company early on.

There is a thinking that comes in learning to manage with little. When a company first starts out, if it has a lot of money, he generally wastes a lot of money on the "wrong" things. At the point that the money runs out, not only does he have to still develop the thinking, but on top of that, he now may have a huge amount of debt to handle as well. This same thing occurs when a company is in a product development phase. If there is too much money available, the focus is on buying, rather than on creating. There is a fine balance between being undercapitalized and overcapitalized during this first phase. These scenarios are neither good nor bad; we are just pointing out a different way of thinking about them.

It is in the second quadrant that the thinking of the leader begins to shift to the other side of the cycle. Typically there is a tipping point of uncertainty where the new focus and thinking (contractive) begins to take hold. As Bill Gates said, often success can be a terrible teacher. It is in this second quadrant that the leader generates the greatest risk for herself in continuing to grow. There comes a realization that the leader has created success and that she has grown something from nothing. It is a point when the leader allows fear to enter her thinking. She discounts the hard work it took, and she begins to wonder if it has all been by luck. In that she is unable to quantify what has taken place to generate this newfound success, she seeks to regain certainty, and thereby her focus and thinking changes.

As a company moves into the third and fourth quadrants, a leader creates a world around himself that is focused on control and stability. As he has driven a level of success, he now realizes he has something, and through the busi-ness and chaos of the creation, he begins the cycle down. He is fearful of loss, as he sees more and more challenges come his way. He will say things like, "How did it come to this? I'm not even sure how we got here. Why does it always have to be like this?" He has now come into a world of problems. He wants to protect his business assets, his people, and the organization as a whole. He now realizes he has something, and loss of it would be failure. He begins to see the obstacles as walls, rather than bridges, and there is a shift in goals, from the growth in the previous phases, to cost savings and other process-improvement-type goals.

Now the business leader has turned her focus to stabilizing and protecting her company, which is a turn of her focus inward. You will hear business owners later in the cycle who are done, and they tell us that they just don't want to do it anymore. These companies can be gems. These are the companies that have become so contractive in their thinking that they literally cannot see opportunity in front of them. These are the leaders who feel they are sacrificing themselves, and think they have for a long period of time.

He will seek the input and assistance of professionals to help chart a course for success. It is important to note when speaking of consultants and their offerings for strategy or planning development, that a strategy, in and of itself, is neither expansive nor contractive in nature. Strategy is merely a direction of focus, a planning initiative that will be used to drive a company to future prospects. In order to understand better the results, ask yourself one simple question: "Is the intention of this strategy one of sales and growth, with the content that will drive you to get the job done? Or alternatively, is the intention of the strategy to drive stabilization and cost reductions in the company?" We are proponents of both. Costs must be controlled in order to drive profitability; however, we know that holding the thinking of one to the exclusion of the other is counterproductive. Strategies need to be weighted toward growth and innovation in order to create new cycles for the company and the leader.

Let us be clear and up front. Should you wish traditional thinking in business, there are many "experts" who can assist you in creating rules for you on what you should and should not do. There are countless systems and solutions available on the market today that certainly solve problems, but at the same time can also create complexity. Remember, the more complex, the more avenues for uncertainty. Perhaps you may have success following their rules; just understand going in what side of the cycle you are working in your thinking.

So, how does the contractive leader create this? Here too are the logical terms and ideas in business and focus, but in them, they drive the natural cycle of contraction. First of all, business owners who have moved to the contractive cycle have largely become dispassionate about their product and servicing the world. She wants to drive productivity and efficiency in her company. She knows that she needs to bring costs down. She wants to get organized, although when asked, she generally doesn't know what that means. She implements complex systems (generally technology based) that promise to provide data for measurement and analysis around aspects of the business that were not considered previously. There is a huge internal focus on training around these new systems. As she drives further into this quadrant and the contraction continues, she cuts more, yielding greater contraction. You get what you give. She has satisfied customers; however, these are not enthusiastic customers. She will say, "If you don't like it, go somewhere else." She will even say, "I don't want those types of customers. My competitors can have them, because they are too much work."

Second to their internal focus on their business is an increased focus on the competitors, and it is generally negative in nature. He sees all the negative sides of his competitors, and he becomes frustrated because in fact they act as a mirror. He stands nothing to learn from them, as he blames them for wrecking a market. The focus on the competitor and the trimming of fat and cost from the organization has replaced the customer- and sales-centered focus. This type of thinking dominates the contractive side of the cycle. Again, you get what you give.

Now, at a micro level, within each phase also exists a pendulum swing; however, in this case, the predominant mode of thinking is between certainty and uncertainty. As we introduced earlier, we all experience a natural swing between certainty and uncertainty in our worlds, in everything we do. It is in fact how we learn and grow as human beings. As you look at a company or business, it is no different. There will be times of certainty and uncertainty as a result of the thinking of the leader(s); this is why we say a company is a reflection of its leadership. Just as computers were developed to think the same way as we do as humans, a company operates and thinks the same way as the leadership. We often smile when we run into a leader who says that he thinks differently from those in his company. In fact, we know that it is not possible. Now sure, he might think differently from an individual within the company on a specific topic, but the general thinking of the company is a reflection of what the leader is thinking.

The company takes direction from the leader, and so if there is a problem, then the leader needs to reflect not only on what he is saying, but on what he is doing. Time and time again, when we talk to the leader of an organization, he will tell us about how this isn't working or that isn't working or his employees are just not getting it. When we ask him what it is he himself truly "gets", he realizes how uncertain he is, and he can see how it is translated into his company. When the leader is certain, we know the company follows. It really is pretty neat, when you think about it.

Now remember these swings within the leader and the company have to occur, because if they didn't, there wouldn't be growth within the company and there wouldn't be any growth for everyone involved. It is the air you breathe in (expansion) that gives life, and the breath out (contraction) that expels the spent residues and prepares you for new air in, and the ultimate new growth that follows. Now wait a minute, this is not business. Business is logical, it is numbers, and it is real-world stuff. That is the convention of it. Those who live solely by convention fight the tides. Those who understand the cycles and remain resilient in their focus, knowing the tides change, are the 10 percent.

Just think about changes you have made in your company. There was a period of uncertainty just before you decided to make a change, and then once you became certain on what needed to be done, you took action to implement the change. If you hadn't had the period of uncertainty, the change would never have occurred, and you would never have grown into the company you are now.

The struggle for most leaders is they fight that feeling of uncertainty. In the fight, they try to push it outside of themselves and put it onto others, but in fact, it is them. You will know what we mean about that feeling of uncertainty. It is those moments of indecision. It is where nothing seems to be working out. It is where you are being pulled in multiple directions. You simply wish everyone would just fall in line, because if they did, then somehow it would be better. Have you ever noticed that it doesn't seem to matter what they do, it doesn't seem to ease the feeling of uncertainty? On the other hand, you know that when you are certain, you can move mountains, and have you ever noticed? So can your employees. Funny how that works, isn't it?

Within each phase, there exists a swing from certainty to uncertainty and back to certainty, as demonstrated in the diagram below:

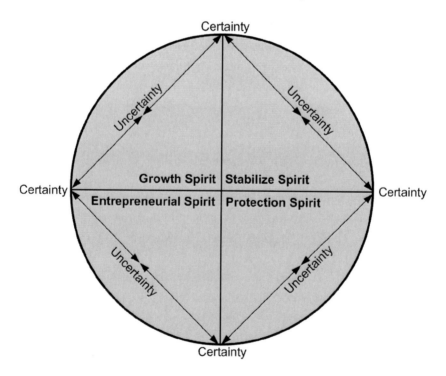

As a company enters one phase, there is certainty, and this is what creates the momentum. Remember, as soon as you are certain in what you need to do, you take action. At some point in each of the phases, there is a point where you become uncertain. There is generally a lot of confusion, doubt, tension, and so on. Then following, there is a decision to go forward or go back in your quest to gain certainty. If you go back, it does not necessarily mean the failure of the company, business, or leader, depending on their strength; however, it will mean there is little, if any, growth for a period of time, until the uncertainty reenters, at which point the swing once again comes into play. This same thing occurs in each phase. The point of uncertainty is required to establish the thinking for the next phase.

For example, think about when you first got into business. At the point you got into business, you were certain about what you were going to do and what you needed to do to establish your business. You had a lot of energy and momentum behind you. At some point, uncertainty entered, when maybe the market didn't respond the way you thought it would, or when you realized how much work it was to operate the business, or when your sales were lower than what you expected, making it difficult to pay your bills. At that point, it was difficult, and there was tension, worry, and anxiety. In fact, you wondered if it was all worth it. At that point, you could have decided it wasn't worth it and gone back to something you knew (certainty). On the other hand, from all of that confusion and uncertainty, you probably decided you needed to do something different. Maybe you refocused your efforts on reaching your market, or maybe you better defined your market. Maybe you decided to learn more about the art of selling to customers and pushed yourself to become better at this. Maybe you went to the bank and changed the terms on a loan. The point just before you took these actions, you would have become certain on what you needed to do to work through the uncertainty, and you took action. As soon as you did these things, you became aware you could grow this business, which propelled your thinking into the next phase.

If you had not had the uncertainty, you would never have had to do something different, and this is where the growth comes in. Even for those who decide it wasn't worth it, in that moment when they go back to something they think is certain, we know chances are they will try again, because they have learned something. This is the reason many people start business after business, or go through periods of fits and starts, until they break through the uncertainty.

Let's look at another example. We worked with a medium-sized company where they had experienced a significant amount of growth. As they described it, their main customer was a large company in the industry, and as other competitors at their level were entering the marketplace, they started to look at product cost cutting to remain competitive. Initially, our client provided these based on the growth projections that were anticipated in the future. Shortly after this, the orders from their customer started leveling off, and they realized they had built more capacity than they needed. As they noticed margins slipping, they became uncertain about a number of things. They questioned the decision around taking on the additional capacity, and they believed it had been a wrong move. They questioned the pricing breaks they had provided their customer, and they questioned the inefficiencies within the operation. We know that as they worked through this uncertainty, they became certain on what they needed to do, which propelled them into the next phase of thinking (contractive). They sold off a number of pieces of equipment. They told their customer they were raising their prices, and they laid off a number of managerial staff and spread the load onto the other managers. What was the result of this?

Well by the time we became involved, their customer was actively looking for a lower-cost supplier, there had been the loss of a number of key employees, and they were still overcapacity for the amount of work they had. However, on the other hand, they did have many of the processes in their operation in line and were making a suitable margin. For the most part, they were solidly in the third phase, and there was a significant amount of fear in the organization around what it would mean if they were to lose their customer. It is easy to see how the uncertainty in this situation had made them take the action that propelled them into the decisions they made. After all, aren't these the things you are told you need to do in conventional business?

Leaders and business owners fall into one of two camps in the conventional business world, in our opinion. On the one side, the leader, while ingrained in the here and now, holds little focus looking out into the future. The problems and uncertainties, present in any given moment, pull her around, and she loses her focus and intention of the future. She is reactive in her need to build certainty, and before long, the shortsighted decisions that she makes propel her into the next quadrant, out of necessity.

On the other side, there are those leaders who, while also ingrained in the here and now, hold a focus and intention for the future. They recognize that the decisions that they make today will impact the future, and they are aware that as they move into the next quadrant, they need to capitalize on this opportunity to reinvest in their growth over the long term. They operationally bridge two quadrants simultaneously, while holding the thinking of the first phase, and in doing so, use the natural momentum to generate growth in different ways.

As you may have guessed by now, we have a tendency to look at the world a little differently. We know that thinking differently allows you to get clear on opportunity and on your intention in business. So we ask, what is your thinking? Are you thinking in the confines of convention? Are you opening up to new ideas? Are you curious and looking for new ideas to expand your thinking? Are you open and innovating and growing? Or are you trying to stabilize yourself, or protect yourself from the world? These are very different root intentions. One holds the premise of expansion, while the other holds the premise of contraction. Quite naturally, your thinking, in and of itself, is the basis for your success as a leader.

Now, how do you get ahead of these swings? In a word … polarization. How congruently and strongly can you maintain your focus? Where is your focus? Are you focused on what you don't want, or on what you do want? How clear are you about what it is that you do want? How much are you swayed by what is happening here and now? How is your own thinking playing out in your organization? Do you allow the death of things, in order to create the life for another? How much are you fighting the natural cycle?

In polarizing and minimizing the tides, and even more, using the tides to move you forward, you will be more successful. As we have discussed, evolution is natural; just look to nature in its power. How many times have men thought they created something greater than nature to overcome a cycle, and how often has nature shown him its utter power and magnificence? Have you ever noticed that many of the greatest inventions are those created by men who took their lead from nature in their creation? Take, for example, Dr. Uri Gat, from Israel, who has manufactured silk from a spider's web. He took the notion from the fact that nature created something extremely strong. In fact, the spider's silk is six times stronger than nylon or steel of the same diameter. Knowing this, the Israeli group went to work to duplicate it, using nature as the example. The result was the potential for lightweight, bulletproof vests, semiconductor chips, optical fibers, textiles, and bandages, to name a few. Take, for example, the study of nature that ultimately created flying machines. Take, for example, Monsanto in its development of biotoxin corn, where they genetically spliced biotoxin into corn to deter bugs. Now, we are not saying all of this development has necessarily been good for everyone, however we believe that in cases where man pushes the envelope, nature will find a way to reset as the pendulum swings.

What are these cycles in nature? They are the seasons, the rain and the dry. They are even the winds, for example; the winds are used by nature. Take, for example, the many moths and butterflies. They cannot survive the freezing temperatures, grounds, and such of the north, so each year they migrate hundreds and in some cases thousands of miles utilizing the jet stream. North winds in summer take them south from the north, and south winds take the warm air and insects north in the new spring season. Of course, these animals have short life spans, but the services they offer each area in their representative season are vital, and so they naturally go with the cycles and flow. Those species that fight this die off as the cold sets in. This is a natural cycle. Have you learned to use the wind in your business? The ten percent of those who consistently make it look easy have the wind at their backs.

In order to get the wind at your back, you must continue to expand your thinking and become aware of the swings and the cycles. You must immerse yourself with those who know, who can share the secrets. We know you can continue to learn and grow on your own; however, find those who can aid you in order to move you along faster. Birds of a feather flock together for a reason.

To get the wind at your back, understand the four keys to polarizing your thinking, to expanding your thinking in an upward spiral, to seeing the world from a higher point, and beginning to observe what is really going on. Ultimately, you will need to understand:

- The only thing you can be certain of is uncertainty.
- Problems and opportunities are constructed the same way.
- Fear is just a construct, and it is not real.
- Your intention, your focus, is the only thing that will create your success.

We will be covering each of these areas in the coming chapters, and probably by this point, you have already begun to think differently about some of them. We promise you will continue to gain new insights and understanding through those chapters in how to change your thinking.

See, you have spent a lifetime living by how the world works, according to the masses. Yet, those masses have not achieved success, so you would think it would be apparently obvious that their thinking is not working. We once read a poster that said if hard work and dedication was all it took to be rich, then the women of Africa would be millionaires. Isn't that true, when you think of it, but isn't that what we have been told to do?

Hopefully, we have started to open the box, but it is up to you whether you have it remain open. Like it or not, you have been programmed to think as you do. It has been going on for years, as you were bombarded by the "rules and convention" of how it is. You are now about to drop a veil of reality into new ways of thinking, a path less taken. Those who experience prosperity are few in the general population. Do they take the same path as the herd?

There Is Certainty Only in Uncertainty

Up to this point, we have talked a lot about the swing between certainty and uncertainty and how it swings us through the phases and the cycle, so let's look at that specifically. The only thing that is absolutely certain is there is always going to be uncertainty. Have you ever noticed that much of the world is made up of dichotomies? There is good and bad, right and wrong, black and white. In reality, we couldn't know one without having known the other. You couldn't know love if you hadn't experienced hate. You couldn't know up if you didn't know down. While each of these sits opposite of the other, there are variations that exist between them. Most of you think one side or the other, in absolutes, it is or it isn't!

Think about the idea of hot and cold. On the one side, if you think about 100 degrees, you would definitively know it was hot; and on the other side, if you thought of -100 degrees, you would know it was cold. If you started on the cold side and started raising the temperature, at which specific point would you move from cold to hot? The same can be said with the sun rising or setting. Is there a specific point when we move from darkness to light? Now there is a convention that states when "x" happens, then that would be considered dark, or when "y" happens, it would be considered light, but there really is no specific point. It is not like there is a light switch that gets flicked on in the morning that moves us from dark to light. There is this in-between, or a variation; however, to truly know one side, you have to have experienced the other. Even when we think of business, you wouldn't know a decline in business if you hadn't known growth, and you certainly wouldn't know profit if you didn't know loss.

There is a level of certainty that exists when you know one side of the pendulum or the other. This is in part why we, as a human race, create rules and convention. It is in the attempt to give us certainty. We like to know what the rules are so that we understand how to operate. When you think about it, without them, things might even be a little chaotic. Can

65

you imagine what it would be like if anyone could drive a car on either side of the street or if seven-year-olds were allowed to get behind the wheel? Can you imagine if there was no such thing as air traffic controllers and planes just took off and flew anywhere they wanted? What if there were no rules of commerce, and once you paid for something, you had to hope that you might get something in return, or that it worked once you received it? Our drive for certainty, in many ways, allows us to operate without having to think much about how the world works. We can all sleep at night, knowing there is a perceived sense of order.

While we strive to create certainty because of the uneasiness uncertainty brings, can you imagine what it would be like if you were absolutely certain of everything? If we, as a people, were absolutely certain of what was going to happen in every given second, then there would be no need to learn and grow. There would be no need for knowledge, because everything that could be known would already be known. Metaphor or not, the story that back in 1843, the US government recommended the patent office be shut down because everything that could possibly be invented was already invented, speaks of certainty of everything. If we were completely certain of everything, we would be as if on remote control, and there would be no need for us to think, there would be no advancement. In fact, we would operate something like robots. There would be no anticipation or excitement. There would be no fear or worry. We would already be certain of the outcome, so nothing could or would surprise us. Is it this type of thinking in the 1800s that drew on nearly a hundred years of few or no inventions of major significance?

There is another school of thought that states everything is uncertain and there is no such thing as certainty. In some realm, this could be true. We don't know what is going to happen from moment to moment. We don't really know if five minutes from now, some asteroid is going to collide with the planet and wipe all of us out, or that a year from now there won't be some terrible disease that results in our demise as a species. Could we, in fact, say that we are certain that this couldn't happen? No; however, there are things we can say that we are pretty certain of. Most of us believe that the sun will come up tomorrow. Most of us believe that in the spring, something will grow from the ground. Most of us believe that at some point in the year, there will be precipitation that will fall from the sky.

While you have a propensity to try to create certainty, remember that certainty and uncertainty are like a pendulum. There has to be a natural swing and momentum to things all around you. Think for a moment about when you were bored. There was a point when you swung so far to one side, it gave you the momentum to get up and do something different. Think about anytime you have made some sort of change in your life. It is when we are at the extremes that it creates the energy to make the change. What about when you decided to get into business? Wasn't there a point when you had had enough of the situation you were in, that drove you to do something different? It was through the momentum that you got enough energy to take on a new challenge and succeed.

As much as you dislike the discomfort of the pendulum swing, you need the swings in order to learn and grow. It is a natural part of how you evolve, and without them, there would be no creativity, no invention, and no progress. At the extremes, you are required to loosen your grip on what you know and believe, in order to let the pendulum swing back the other way. It is in the extremes you generally feel the greatest amount of conflict internally, as you consider what is true in what you know and believe. We are required to question your thinking and to see things in a different way. Generally, once you free yourself to think in a different way, you can let go of the conflict, find clarity, and pick up momentum to swing the other way. The truth is, all truths are but half truths, all truths are but half false. Once you realize there are no poles, and that certainty is only uncertainty and they only differ in degree, you can utilize the swings.

Let's see what this looks like with a simple example. For each of us, there are things we are absolutely certain of at given times of our lives. For example, maybe you are living in a home right now that you are happy with and have no intention of leaving. If this is the case, you know where it is located. You know how to drive to work. You know where you have stored things in the house, and I will tell you that you certainly know the quickest way of cleaning it. In this case, you don't think a lot about it, and it probably doesn't come up in conversation much. We have all had these times in our life when we are certain. However, one day the thought enters that maybe you should consider moving. It might have been that you saw a new home that sparked your interest. It might have been the news that you were going to have a new baby. It could have been you had to wait too long for the one bathroom in your current home. There was this moment when the thinking opened up for you; and in that instant, all of a sudden, you started the process of rationalizing your beliefs and ideas about your home. The moment before that, you were absolutely certain in what you knew, but then you started thinking.

You started noticing the little things you don't like about your current house. As you were driving home from work, you started noticing "For Sale" signs. You started looking at your finances and visiting the Internet to see what type of mortgage you could afford. You were consciously and unconsciously debating with yourself back and forth about whether or not you should make a move. You may have talked different ideas over with your friends to try to ease the conflict, but we know you knew that it was still there. At some point in the conflict, you will have made a decision that you were staying or that you were moving, and in making that decision, you allowed the pendulum to swing. You will have let go of the thinking and just moved to taking action, because in this case, you were certain on what you needed to do. At that point, it will have become clear you needed to do some fix up on your current house, or to hire a real estate agent. Whatever supported the new belief. Now, we all know the physical work involved in selling, fixing up, or moving can be immense; however, once your decision was clear and you were certain, the conflict will have subsided related to this decision.

While we used the example of deciding to change homes, this same thing happens both at a micro and macro level in terms of individually, in companies, and in society. This same thing can and will happen in terms of, say, the decision of how much work you are going to do to fix up the house before you put it on the market. The conflict could be on whether to paint, or whether to replace baseboards, and so on. It is a natural part of how we evaluate, but it is in the process of evaluation we feel the most uncertainty and experience the most conflict. While some of this conflict will be conscious, some of it will be unconscious; however, if you didn't have this, you wouldn't progress.

If we look at our society, there have been times we have undergone extreme conflict in order to change our society's beliefs. At one point in time, it was believed smoking was actually good for you, and now as a society, we believe the opposite. There was a time when we believed the world was flat, and although there was much opposition to the idea at the time that it wasn't, now we know something quite different. At one time, it was believed no one would ever have the need for a personal computer, and yet today, most of us have a hard time leaving them. In the past, there was a belief you would work for the same company for the rest of your life.

Monumental events can change a society's thinking in an instant. For example, take the 9-11 tragedy. Until that point in time, the United States believed that conflict of that nature could not occur on their soil. In the days right after, there was an incredible amount of uncertainty that spread through the people of North America. There were questions of, is there another threat imminent? Am I and my family safe? What will this mean for the economy? It required all Americans to question what they had been certain of prior to that moment, and uncertainty was created in their new thinking. Once the shock subsided, there was a change of beliefs that resulted in different actions being taken. Security was strengthened at the borders. A plan to invade the enemy was put in place. Resources of all kinds were engaged to protect the citizens at home and abroad. The pendulum swung, and action was taken and is still being taken in support of the new thinking. There was certainty in what was being done, and that created the momentum to move forward.

In the next chapter, we talk about how you create problems and opportunities in your thinking. Part of the evaluation of uncertainty is what has you construct the problems and the opportunities, and in many cases, you need to make them up in order to drive back to certainty. We know, at this point, that may seem foreign to you—the concept of making things up. We like to tell ourselves that children make things up, but in fact we all do. You have no other choice when it comes to getting clear on what you believe, and we delve further into this in the coming chapter.

This moves us to the next point. Most of us will have heard about the cause and effect equation. It is the concept that when something happens (a cause), it will have an effect on something else. We see it in action all the time. For example, if you decide to reduce the number of salespeople in your company (cause), your expenses will go down (effect). If you decide to sell an asset (cause), you will impact your financial statement (effect). This principle is at play all the time. There is nothing that you can do, say, or think that will not have an effect on the outside world. You are a powerful projection in the world, although you often don't recognize it. As a leader, everything you do, say, or think will be impacting your company and its employees, customers, supply chain, and so on. This is something leaders often forget because they think of themselves as ordinary people; however, just by the position they hold, they impact a great many people's thinking.

In order to change your company, you need to change your thinking, and one of the places to start is in terms of cause and effect. There are countless people around you who believe that they are at effect to things around them. You will hear things like, "I can't get the project done, because I don't have the information. I would have cleaned up that report, but you didn't tell me what you wanted. I would have bid on that job, but there wasn't enough time." At times, this can be frustrating for a leader in an organization, but one of the things we will ask is, how are you creating this? That's right; as a leader, how are you creating these people behaving as they are?

You are probably thinking, what do you mean, how do I create this? I don't. Just for a moment, what if you did? The two of us hold a convenient belief, which works for us. We believe that we are at cause for or that we consciously or unconsciously create everything that is happening or not happening in front of us in any given moment. Certainly anyone can debate whether this is true or not, but just for a second, think about what it would do for you if you chose, now, to adopt this belief. There will have been times when you thought to yourself, "He makes me so angry." Now let us ask you, are you in charge of how you feel? Isn't that your choice? We don't dispute that another person might have done something, but it is up to you to choose how to interpret it and to choose how to feel about it. Can someone else make you feel anything if you don't want to?

We know some of you will be saying, "Yeah, but I can't control everything." One of our favorite examples is the economy. We will be asked, "So, how am I at cause for that?" Right now, as long as you are at effect to the economy, you are feeling a prisoner to something outside of you and you are stuck. What if you switched your thinking to the idea that somehow you created it? How could it change your thinking? As long as you believe something is happening *to* you, it is hard to be creative in coming up with different ideas, because you feel uncertain and powerless. Remember, as soon as you are certain, you create the momentum to move. In thinking about it as if you created it, you can ask yourself a different set of questions. If you have had a downturn in business, ask yourself, "How did I do this?" It could have been you reduced your sales force instead of investing in training to take on more business. It could have been you didn't introduce a new line of products. It could have been you didn't expand to a new market. In looking at it this way, you have a lead on what you could do to turn it around. Remember, there are companies that experience significant growth even in the face of industry decline. What do they do differently?

A company we worked with experienced this exact scenario. They started seeing reduced sales from their present clients, and started the process of eliminating expenses, including trimming their sales force. At first, the leader was resistant to the idea of getting at the cause. He was looking to blame everything outside of the company for the reasons he had taken the actions he took. As we worked with him and he changed his thinking, he began to believe that maybe he had created the reduced sales. He knew there were other customers he wanted to go after, but had been afraid to do so because, at the time, he was close to capacity and he wasn't sure he could take them on. In that moment, he changed the direction of his focus. He hired leading salespeople in the field, who had been laid off from his competitors, he addressed the speed of design and prototyping, and he invested in some additional capacity to augment his existing service offerings. In taking these steps, he was able to secure contracts with the customers he wanted to go after, and his business continued to grow, even though a number of his competitors were dissolved through the 2008 market meltdown.

If that leader had chosen to remain at effect to everything outside of him, it would not have been possible for him to see the opportunity. He would have remained stuck. His organization and people would have remained stuck, and his customers would have suffered. Being at effect to something outside of you creates uncertainty within you and puts you in a loop that can be hard to get out of. It creates conflict, and it creates stuck. It is uncomfortable and feels incredibly unproductive. Remember, when we get clear and certain on something, we create a lot of energy and are able to get a lot of work done in a short period of time.

Again, we ask leaders how they are creating people being at effect in their organization. We know that generally when a company is struggling, it is the person at the top who is leading the charge in that type of thinking. Steve Jobs was quoted as saying, "The people who are crazy enough to think that they can change the world, are the ones that actually do." As long as you as a leader are at effect to the world, then you have not moved over to the thinking that will allow you to change your present circumstances and therefore change your world. If you can't do that for you, how can you hold the intention and actualize it through others in your organization?

In terms of certainty and uncertainty related to cause and effect, something else that needs to be considered is our emotional state. Now some will believe that your emotional state is driven by the circumstances that are present in any given moment. As we mentioned, there are those who believe they are at effect to their emotional state; they say, "He makes me angry" or "When she does this, it really frustrates me." On the other hand, in an instant, we can feel confident and happy when things work out the way we planned. Each and every day, we are faced with a barrage of information requiring us to make interpretations, and in that process, we either consciously or unconsciously choose an emotional state.

You yourself know that when you are in a great mood, things seem easy, and you can get a lot of work accomplished. On the other hand, we are sure you have noticed times when you are in a negative state, and nothing seems to go right. This happens to all of us; however, in adopting the thinking of being at cause, recognize you are in control of your thinking, and by association, your state.

So why is this important, you might ask? Well, our state has an impact on how certain or uncertain you feel in any given moment, and it actually impacts your ability to think. Have you ever noticed that when you are in a powerful state, such as being happy or confident, you are able to process information faster and to make decisions easily? When you are in a negative state, your processing of information and your ability to make decisions are slowed down and completely limited in nature.

When you are uncertain, you often experience negative states, such as guilt, sadness, worry, and fear. On the other hand, when you are certain, you experience the flip side of the coin. You are happy, confident, powerful, and so on. When you are uncertain about something, you actually forget the tools and resources that you have to bring to the table. For a moment, just think of a time when you were uncertain about something and remember what kind of state you were in. Did you notice in that moment, it was difficult to see a solution? Maybe you walked away from the situation for a moment and someone told you something really funny, or maybe something else happened to pull you from that state, and in that moment, the solution presented itself. Our state is a huge contributing factor to our level of certainty or uncertainty, and yet for many people, they believe it is the other way around.

Think about this in your home life. How many times have you come home, maybe in a bad mood, from things that have gone on at work? As soon as you walk in the door, you start complaining about how this person or that person didn't do what you asked him or her to do. Or, you complained about how a customer was being unreasonable. If you were lucky, your loving family listened to you, and then your son or daughter climbed on your lap and told you he or she loves you and put a big smile on your face. As soon as that happened, you became certain of something, which transferred over to your ability to solve the struggles of the day. If this has happened, please hug your family back, because they are helping you to recover the resources and tools that already exist within you to work through anything.

As a society, we have a tendency to get caught up in the loop of, "Well, I have a bigger problem than you." They stand at the watercooler and try to outdo each other as they complain about what is happening to them. One person starts off and says that he had a disagreement with his wife over painting the kitchen. The other person says, "Yeah, well, my kids are skipping school and not listening." The next person says, "I can top that," as she tells you about some issue she is having at the bank. We see this all the time. This is uncertainty at play. This is negative emotional state at play. Everyone is climbing into the same boat, and before long, everyone is stuck in their perceived problem and feeling terrible about it. It only takes a moment to pull you and the people around you out of the problem. If all of a sudden, something makes everyone laugh or someone comes in with exceptional news, then how people see the world will change in that instant.

Think about the meetings you attend. Just by their very nature, meetings have a tendency to be focused on trying to build certainty within a group. Generally when everyone is certain, then there is little need for them to exist. Now, we believe that meetings can be a good thing, if they are in fact bringing about certainty. This said, more times than not, when we sit in on the meetings at our clients, we find that the state is often not conducive to doing this. Everyone comes in at best with a neutral state, and some come in with a negative state. In those instances when there is someone who is positive, it doesn't seem to take long, and the next thing you know he is dragged down as well, and if anything there becomes more uncertainty in the room. Remember, a leader is often the most powerful projection in the room and has the greatest ability to change the state. If she is not in a state that will pull certainty, then without a doubt, the rest of the group will follow. There have been numerous attempts to try to build certainty into the meeting process, with the use of agendas and minutes, but there has to be the thinking behind these tools to make them effective.

So, let's recap the thinking we have been talking about in this chapter. First of all, there are some beliefs that we encourage you to adopt, right now:

- Choose to believe that you are at cause for everything that is happening in front of you, right now.
- Choose to believe that you are at cause for your emotional state.
- Choose to believe that you have far more tools and resources available to you when you are feeling powerful, and that by having access to those, you will create more certainty for yourself and your organization.

Take the first step by recognizing this information and type of thinking did not simply fall into your hands. Be at cause for the fact that you manifested it for you and your organization, right now. You were in search of a different way of thinking about what you want to create, either consciously or unconsciously, and because of that, you are at cause for seeking the answers that you need to do so, right now. Be at cause when it comes to applying this thinking, and be certain that in doing so and in continuing to expand your beliefs and thinking in this area, we will create the certainty that will drive momentum in your organization.

In order to create more certainty for you and your organization, challenge yourself to create more certainty for yourself and your employees, purposefully. The first step is to control your own state. These are the things we tell our clients when we are working with either the leader or the management team:

- Recognize that you make a choice on your emotional state in any given moment. You can choose to feel anger, sadness, or worry, or you can choose to feel powerful, confident, and happy. One of the fastest ways to change a state is to find the humor in things. The second is to notice your own physiology. If you want to feel more confident, then pull your shoulders back, lift your head, and take a deep breath. Think of a time in the past when you felt totally confident, and as you think of that time, notice how your state changes. The same thing works for happiness, power, and so on.
- Recognize that when you control your state, you will influence your employees' state, and in doing, so you will move them from thinking slowly and methodically to thinking more creatively.

The second step is to solidly plant your thinking on the cause side of the equation. Notice when you are creating "convenient excuses" and when you are blaming things outside yourself for where you are right now.

- Every time you see something that is disagreeable, ask yourself this simple question, "How did I create this?" The wording here is specific, so please take note. It is not, "Why did I create this?" It is, "How did I create this?" When we ask why, we are only making up more reasons and excuses, and it isn't helpful to the process.

The third step is to build on the thinking you now have around problems and opportunities, which will be discussed in the next chapter. Remember the only way we can have a problem or an opportunity is to future pace a current circumstance or situation. Part of what creates uncertainty is our own evaluation of options, however remember, in reality you are making them up in your head. Recognize there is far less uncertainty when you stay on the cause side of the cause and effect equation. As long as you are in your box of thinking, that is what is driving the uncertainty and the conflict that you are feeling. As you continue on through the next few chapters, we are going to continue to build your thinking around staying at cause.

Now, here is a word of caution on this type of thinking. First of all, as you read this, you will have remembered instances where you noticed what we have been talking about. As you go out into the world, you will begin to notice even more. You will notice where others are at effect to things outside of them. You will notice how others' emotional state gets in the way of developing solutions. You will see the flow between certainty and uncertainty, and you will want to point it out to the people around you. It is a natural part of the way you learn and grow, so we respect that and we respect you; however, the first step begins with you as the leader.

Oftentimes you will try to fix things that are outside of you. You know, those people who point out everything that is wrong or who tell you that you should do this to fix that. As long as you are pointing at things outside of yourself, you are still working on the effect side of the equation. The question needs to be, "How am I creating this?" Recognize how what you are doing is creating that in others. In terms of leadership, we believe this is what makes the difference between managers and leaders. Managers try to manage others, while leaders inspire others through their own action, through their resolve, and through their accountability for everything that is happening in their organization. Choose to lead, and leave the managing for your competition.

Problems versus Opportunities

Problems and opportunities are constructed in the same way. You just haven't been taught to see the similarities, and therefore you believe they are different. You also believe the differences are real.

We know that you are probably reading this and thinking, "What are you talking about? Of course, they are different, and they are definitely real." Just for a moment consider, what if they were the same? What if a problem wasn't really a problem, and therefore it wasn't real? What if you could change your thinking in an instant and see an opportunity instead? What would that do for you and your company?

Our world is filled with what most of you believe are problems. In fact, most of society talks about their problems. In the media, we will hear about the economic problems, about the health care problems, about the problems with our government and our politicians, and so forth. When you get around the watercooler, you hear about the problems with the boss, about the issues that are going on with the computer systems, about how the customer is placing more demands on you. When you get home, you hear about the problems in school, about the broken dishwasher, about the challenge in coordinating schedules. Just listen around you about the number of problems that exist. We are a world of problems. That is in your focus.

As a result, you seek out training in problem solving, you read books on problem solving, and you evaluate your managers on their abilities to problem solve. Many of you have bought into your value being linked with how well you are able to problem solve. Over the years, society has even moved to the concept of creative problem solving. The study of problem solving as a concept is relatively new. In 1935, Karl Duncker wrote the book *The Psychology of Productive Thinking*, in which he discussed that the difficulty in solving a problem arises from the functional fixedness of the elements that form to construct the problem. Some of you may have heard or seen his candle problem, where he would provide participants with a candle, a box of tacks, and a book of matches, with the instructions that they were to affix the candle to the wall, only using these elements and without lighting the candle. The participants would struggle with how this was to be done, and most times would believe that the problem was not solvable. In order to solve the problem, participants had to see the functionality of the box used to store the tacks in a different way. If they emptied the tacks and used the box as a shelf, they were able to affix the box to the wall, using the tacks, and then place the candle inside. The difficulty of this problem arises from the functional fixedness of the tack box. It is a container in the problem situation, but must be used as a shelf in the solution situation.

Study in this area was revived in the sixties and seventies and has yielded variations on different problem-solving techniques and strategies, such as brainstorming, hypothesis testing, lateral thinking, root cause analysis, trial and error, and so on. While each of these may solve a problem, we know that in order to construct a problem, there is a mechanics involved.

In the book *Flow: The Psychology of Optimal Experience*, Mihaly Csikszentmihalyi wrote that we are only able to process approximately 134 bits of information from the 2 million bits of information that are presented to us in any given second. We are surrounded with information, such as the color of the walls, the noises around us, the feelings of our bodies, and more, but it is through the process of deleting, generalizing, and distorting this information that we are able to consciously identify those things that are important to us, and in that second, we give meaning to that information. For example, have you ever been looking for a set of keys, and after you have looked all over, someone points out they are on the table, right in front of you? The keys were always there, but through the processing of information being presented to you in your mind, you deleted the presence of them in that second. As soon as you are consciously made aware of their location by someone else, you are able to see them.

We process the 2 million bits of information based on our own internal filters. These filters are comprised of things such as our beliefs, our values, decisions, and so on. We filter out the information that we deem to be unnecessary, and instead we focus on what we believe to be the critical details in any given second. The portion of the brain that is attributed to this filtering is referred to as the Reticular Activating System, or RAS. It bridges the lower part of the brain, which performs automatic functions like breathing, to the upper part of the brain, where thought occurs. It is said to be the gateway between external stimuli and cognition.

When you enter into a new situation, the first thing you notice is what you have trained your brain to unconsciously scan for. Without realizing it, you experience what you intend to experience. You interpret your world based on what you have experienced in the past and based on what you believe about yourself. One of the things that we often tell our clients is to be aware of what you are training your employees on. A case in point is the training around conflict management. Many companies will spend time, money, and energy on training their management to resolve conflict. After they have undertaken this training, we ask them whether the amount of conflict in the organization has increased or decreased. In almost 100 percent of the cases, the level of conflict in the organization will have increased. Why is that? Well, when you learn new tools and techniques, you inherently want to apply what you have learned. In order to do this, you need to see opportunities to do so, and therefore you are unconsciously attuned to look for this information. It is a natural part of who you are, and so in taking on the beliefs that conflict needs to be resolved and that you have the answer, you have to start to notice its presence around you.

We all take on beliefs about who we are, and in doing so, we filter the information around us in support of those beliefs. Teachers will see students who need to be taught. Safety professionals will see the potential for accidents. Electricians will notice burned-out lightbulbs. Doing so concretes your beliefs that you are needed and valuable in what you do.

The same happens when you think about yourself being a good problem solver. Everybody knows that in order to be a good leader, you need to be a good problem solver, or so you have been told. It is something that has been written about over and over. When you focus on the successes of other companies and leaders, it is often attributed to them being able to solve a problem. However, as you think about that, if this were really the case, what would you have to see? That's right. You would have to see the problems all around you.

As you filter the 2 million bits of information that come in through your senses into the approximately 134 bits you consciously process, you give a meaning to that information, and doing so unconsciously drives your emotional state and your behavior. When you see something pleasing, you may smile, laugh, or respond by thanking or congratulating someone. In the opposite case, if you determine something is unsatisfactory, you may respond quite differently. In most cases, we are unconscious to our responses, although they are driven by how we filter the information around us. Have you ever had a situation where you and a coworker have attended the same meeting and heard someone say something different? After the meeting, as you compared notes, you realized you came out with entirely different interpretations of what was said. These are your own personal filters at play. One of you will hold different beliefs, values, intentions, and experiences from the other, and as a result, pick up different information from a common experience.

In the Star Trek universe, the Vulcans were able to perform the Vulcan "mind meld," a technique used in sharing thoughts, experiences, memories, and knowledge with another individual. While our lives would certainly be easier on many fronts if we were able to do so, at this point in our evolution, we have yet to be able to perform such a feat. The way in which we convey our thoughts and ideas, based on our interpretation of the world, to those around us, is through our physiology and our language.

Language, in and of itself, is an interesting study. An individual could spend years exploring semantics and the evolution and the meaning of language; however, for the purpose of this book, there are a couple of principles that are important to understand. The first one is to understand how imprecise language is in conveying your thoughts and ideas. In order to demonstrate, if I were to ask you to imagine a bike in your mind, and at the same time, I also imagined a bike in mine, what are the chances that our two pictures would match? In all likelihood, they wouldn't, although we could both be talking about a bike, thinking that we were talking about the same thing, when in fact nothing could be further from the truth.

While this is a simple example, this is happening around you all of the time. How often have you been having a conversation with someone, believing that you are in agreement around something, only to find out that the other person did something entirely different in the end? How many times have you thought you were going to receive a report on something, only to receive something entirely different? How many times have you had a rule put in place, only to find that someone interpreted it a different way? Is there any wonder our lawbooks and policy manuals are so long? There have been many times when we have had clients tell us that communication within their company is an issue, and we agree with them, simply understanding how imprecise language really is. The words we use can only be interpreted based on our own experience; however, we use our same personal experience to interpret what someone else is saying, and therein lies the disconnect.

In our use of language, there is an interpretation that we unconsciously make in selecting the words we use to describe our world. At the same time we are using words to describe what we are talking about, you are in fact building an internal representation (or pictures, sounds, smells, tastes) of what we mean. For example, if you are talking to our coworkers about solving a problem, whether consciously or unconsciously, you have built an internal representation of what you are in fact talking about; however, you are using words to describe it. The cruelty in this is that no matter how you try to describe something using words, the imprecision of language will never allow you to adequately describe what you have constructed in your mind.

Think about trying to describe the taste of an orange to someone who has never tasted one. How could you possibly describe the sweet taste, or the tang, or the refreshing flavor of an orange and do it justice? Words are not adequate to describe any complete experience. They are limited in what they can convey. In order for me to work through the process of trying to understand what you are saying, I need to build my own internal representation, based on my own beliefs and experiences. We know these can be so vastly different from yours that in making our individual interpretations of what is being said, we can miss each other entirely in our attempt to describe the world around us. If you were to tell me the orange had a citrus flavor, I would have to search back into my bank of memories to a time when I tasted something with a citrus flavor and attempt to match what you are saying with that idea. This process is called building a complex equivalence and is mostly unconscious in our thinking. You are continually looking for certainty, and part of this is doing a comparison between what is in front of you now and what you have experienced in the past. While you are aware that your description of citrus is the flavor of an orange, mine could be of a lemon, resulting in an entirely different idea of what an orange really is, had I never tasted one.

Now in some cases, when we have had a shared experience, the words we use to describe that experience can encompass greater meaning. When we talk about the people who were present or about the person who was wearing the red hat or about what was discussed, we have a context that is similar, so there are fewer variables for error, although even that does not ensure accuracy. We often fool ourselves into believing that you know what other people are telling you when they use words to describe their experience; however, the point here is that there is really no way of knowing that you really know what someone else is saying. The irony in all of this is that even in reading this book, there is no way that you can really know specifically what we are talking about or what specifically we mean. The best that you can do is to interpret what you are reading based on your own filters of experience and beliefs. In doing so, you will make sense of this information in your own way. We have all heard the saying that there are three sides to every story, and now you know that there are as many sides to any story as there are people to talk about it. Anytime we are conveying a message or a story using words, it is open for interpretation by not only the speaker, but the observer and the listener.

So now that we have laid the groundwork, I am sure you are asking yourself, "How is all this important to how problems and opportunities are constructed?" First of all, let me say that it is simply in the thinking. There are no such things as problems, and by association, the same can be said for opportunities. We know that you know people, who only seem to have problems; however, this doesn't have to be the case. Our world is full of opportunity. It just requires you to see that potential in holding what you know to be true, right in front of you, now. Know that thesis and antithesis are identical in nature, only different in degree. So the paradox of the problem and opportunity equation rests in the same realm of thinking. A problem and opportunity are exactly the same; they only differ in degree.

In order to construct a problem or an opportunity, there is simply one thing you are doing in your minds. You take a present circumstance or condition, put it into the future, and in doing so, make a determination about whether it is a problem or an opportunity. By the way, please let us be clear that you are making it up in your minds. There is no way that we really know what is going to happen thirty seconds from now, never mind an hour, a week, a month, or a year from now. In order to make the evaluation that you have a problem or an opportunity right now, you need to consider how it will play out in the future. As soon as you make this determination, it can provide you with the certainty on what we need to do or give us direction. On the other hand, it can also place you in a loop, if you are not clear on your focus.

In order to demonstrate how this works, let's run through a couple of examples of how problems are presented, and then we can talk about the mechanics of what we do to construct them. Let's start with an example of a dog barking. Your friend might come up to you and say something like, "My dog barks too much." Now, a dog barking in and of itself is not a problem. It is a natural thing that a dog might bark, and in fact, there are probably times when a barking dog could be a good thing. In order to have this as a problem, your friend must be considering when this would, in fact, cause an issue in the future. He might be thinking about this when he has visitors to his home, who are then greeted by a barking dog. He might be thinking about this in terms of being awakened in the middle of the night when the dog barks. He might be thinking when the dog barks, the people around him might think that his dog has misbehaved. In all of these situations, he has identified a current circumstance or condition and then future paced it, in order to identify "My dog barks too much" as a problem. If he had not future paced it, he could not have identified it as a problem.

Have you ever had a time when someone has told you about a problem, and in listening to how she describes it, you have identified how in fact she could resolve the issue? You give her your sound advice, only to find out that she hasn't taken it. Well, now you know the reason. In most cases, you talk about a problem in the here and now. Remember, when you are listening to others describe a situation, you build an internal representation of what they are telling you, and as soon as you think you have it, you give them our advice. In building your own internal representation of the problem, you naturally do your own future pacing of the present circumstance or situation and base your advice on that. Your friend may have future paced it in an entirely different way, so your advice doesn't solve the problem for her. In the case of the dog barking, for example, your friend might have future paced the circumstance with being awakened, whereas you paced it forward with being greeted by the barking dog. Your advice to your friend was, "I wouldn't worry about it; your dog doesn't bark that much, and he is really friendly." Can you see how what you gave for advice didn't fit the future pace, and why it might be easy to disregard the advice that others give you when it is not assisting us in solving our future-pace perception of the problem?

Now, before we go onto another example, there is another point we need to make about problems and opportunities. The best way to think about them is as convenient excuses. They are either the reason you do something or the reason you don't do something, and the words *problem* and *opportunity* are interchangeable. In some cases, you have to see problems in order to work through solutions, and the same can be said for opportunities. In other situations, you need to see the opportunities. At the end of the day, they are just simply convenient excuses. They provide us with a reason for doing whatever you think you should do, and that is wonderful when they are motivating you to move forward. If you are doing something to fix a problem or to go after an opportunity, that is great; however, many people get stuck in the excuses and they don't go anywhere. In a future chapter, we will discuss the topic of intention, and you will see how building and holding a strong intention allows to you find success in a different way.

Let's look at another example. In working with our clients, one of the things we hear frequently is about the problem of finding skilled labor. In a large majority of the cases, when we ask our client if they have the staff and skills to complete the work today, they will tell us that they do, but that this is still a problem. We ask in what circumstances this will be the case, and they tell us that it is a problem in expanding their business, in addressing their years of experience as the baby boomers retire, in entering new markets, and so on. They have had to future pace skilled labor into the future in order to determine it is a problem today. If they didn't want to consider expanding their business or strengthening their business, then they wouldn't see it as a problem today. Remember that problems and opportunities are constructed the same way, and at their core, they are just convenient excuses. As we dig a little deeper, we find that our clients' real concerns are around whether or not they should expand into new markets, how they should restructure their workforce, how they could be utilizing technology, and so on. More times than not, it is these unconscious issues that are the root of how a problem is constructed. Generally speaking, the problem presented is typically not the real issue. The answer lies in addressing these real issues, not in the skilled labor.

We have all heard that we need to "think outside the box." A problem or opportunity is simply a box. In constructing the box, you hinge belief on belief based on your experience, and these beliefs make up the sides of the box. As you look at a problem or opportunity, you future pace your present circumstances, and as you do so, you strengthen your resolve that you do in fact have a box. The challenge is in being able to think beyond the box. In the case of the skilled labor, when you look at all the variables that need to be considered, you unconsciously future pace them to evaluate whether you are ready to take on an opportunity; but in doing so, they suddenly become a problem that you talk about as if it is in the now.

One of the beliefs we hold for our clients, our students, and those people around us, is that they have the skills, resources, knowledge, and know-how to overcome any perceived problem or opportunity, once they are clear on what thinking has created it. In the case of skilled labor, we discovered that their real issue was about whether or not to expand to another market. Skilled labor may in fact be a consideration, but on the front side of the box, it becomes the convenient excuse for not moving forward. Once you decide you will expand to a new market, you can and will expand your thinking to evaluate training opportunities, process structure, organization structure, and so on. When you become certain in your decision, there are always ideas, current strengths, and thinking that will come into play that will have you think outside of the box.

At the beginning of this chapter, we stated that problems and opportunities are not real, and what we mean in saying this is that, as we have discussed, they are constructed in your mind when you pace a current situation forward. As soon as you lock them in time, you lock your own self into the thinking that they are real, and expend a lot of energy in discussing something that only exists in your mind. We know you will know what we are talking about in looking around and seeing how much our society engages in discussion around their problems. The more power you give to a problem being real, the more you take away from your own abilities to see the opportunity. It was Warren Buffet who said, "Be fearful when others are greedy. Be greedy when others are fearful." In order to do this, you need to be aware that a present circumstance has the ability to be both a problem and an opportunity, and it is up to you how you choose to see it. The more you listen to problems and believe they are real, the more problems you will see and the more you will believe they exist.

Case in point, if we look at the present global economic downswing, there are numerous people on the street and in the media who talk about how many problems there are in the way of starting new businesses and expanding into new markets. They talk about the uncertainty in the world and about how unstable things are, and they are right. There certainly are people who are uncertain because they have bought into the thinking that everything is a problem. Are there people who are making money right now? You bet. Are there companies that are expanding into new markets? You bet. Are there companies who see this as an opportunity to position themselves for growth in the future? Absolutely. If you choose to buy into your problems and make them real, they will define your path in the future.

We have all experienced this type of opposite thinking at times; however, one of the things we want to do is bring this to conscious awareness so you can utilize this process in your everyday life. We have all had times when we believed that something was a problem, but once we got you going, you found out that in fact it wasn't or you found that what you believed was a problem was easier to solve than you could have understood at the beginning. We have the skills and resources required; however, they are easy to forget about when you climb into a box of a problem.

So, let's recap the thinking that we have been talking about in this chapter. First of all, there are some beliefs that we encourage you to adopt, right now:

- Problems and opportunities are constructed the same way, in your mind.
  - o In order to have either, you need to take a present circumstance or situation and future pace it.
  - o At the point where you future pace it, you make a determination on whether it is a problem or an opportunity, and you talk about it as if it is in the present, locking it in time.
  - o Problems and opportunities are only real in your own mind, and you have the ability to see either one, in an instant.
- Problems and opportunities are just convenient excuses for doing or not doing what you want to do.
- We have all the skills, resources, knowledge, and know-how to overcome any obstacle, once you are clear about what is important to us.

Remember that in order to give ourselves direction, we are always future pacing our ideas of the world. You take what circumstances are present in the here and now and consider those same circumstances in the future. This is a natural part of who you are, and if you didn't do this, then chances are you wouldn't get out of bed in the morning. The one downfall is that in order to do this, you need to make up scenarios, in your mind, that may or may not be true. It is the culmination of our experiences and beliefs that filter your thinking; however, just because something has happened in our past does not mean you are destined to repeat it. The amazing thing about us as humans is that you have the capacity to learn and grow from these experiences, but you often forget that you do. In fact, it is only when you do not learn from your experiences that you must repeat them.

In order to "think outside the box," you need to be able to recognize what thinking you have employed to create that box. You may have trained your mind to think in a specific way, so initially this may take a little time to work through; however, this is easy to do. Once you have retrained the way your mind works, you will be able to do this on the fly. Simply following these steps will allow you to see things from a different perspective:

- As soon as you believe you have a problem or opportunity, get clear on what your intention is, or where you are trying to get to, or what you are trying to do in the future. Write this down in front of you. In essence, this is your goal or end point.
- Ask yourself if this is really what *you* want to do. There are lots of times when others will tell you what you should do, but it is not what you really want to do. Be clear that this is something you want for you or your company. Let others figure out what is good for them. If it is something *you* want, then proceed; and if not, then either define what you want or let it go, noticing that it was nothing.
- If it is something you want, then look at the problem or opportunity from the vantage point of an outsider. List all of the resources, skills, knowledge, and know-how that you would see if you were looking at this from an outside point of view. If you like, think of yourself as a friend who is giving advice to someone whom you intimately know.
  o   Note: In order to be effective in this, you need to let go of

your thinking around it being a problem, and you need to look for the opportunities. Remember, a problem isn't real. You are making it up, so since you are doing so, make up an opportunity instead.

- Identify the first thing that you will need to do, in order to take the very first step that will allow you to ultimately reach your intention.

Remember the point of all of this is to change your thinking. Sometimes we will have clients and students who will spend the time defending their way of thinking, and the only thing we will ask them is, "How is it working for you?" We respect that each of you likes to do things your own way, and if the way you resolve problems and seek out opportunities is working for you, then by all means, please keep thinking the way you are thinking. In our experience, those who have adopted and recognized this different way of looking at the world and how we think have been able to quickly identify what in the past were obstacles and to clear those away faster and more efficiently.

Imagine for a moment, the value you would have to your organization if you could employ this type of thinking. Doesn't it give some different thoughts about what is possible?

Fear

As I am sure you are starting to recognize, you do an incredible number of things in our minds. You create problems, opportunities, certainty and uncertainty for yourself, simply in how you choose to interpret the information that is being presented to you in any given moment.

We discussed how your emotions drive your thinking. When you are in a negative state, you tend to be slower and more linear in your thinking, while when we are in a positive state, we access the tools and resources that make our thinking more intuitive and experiential-based. We are clear that in business, you need to have the flexibility to access both kinds of thinking. There are times when you will want to be more logical and methodical; however, when you get caught in a box, we also know the steps to effectively pull yourself out in order to get a different result.

We are sure you will agree as a business leader that there are times when you just have to be able to "trust your gut." There will be numerous examples in your own experience when you have done exactly that, and in doing so, have found success. If not, you are missing out on a strength you were designed to use. Of course, there will have also been those times when maybe the opposite was true and you used logical thinking to work through an idea. You generally strengthen your thinking, one way or the other, based on the success that we have had in either camp; however, your strength as a business leader will be in your ability to manage your own flexibility in accessing either.

In the business world, you are told to manage by the numbers. You have accounting systems, marketing plans, business plans, bankers, laws, and regulations. Consultants will tell you that your focus needs to be on the logical aspect of running your business. Of course, there needs to be a focus on this; however, many of today's most successful business leaders discuss the importance of being able to trust their intuition as well.

The late Steve Jobs said in his recently published biography, "I began to realize that an intuitive understanding and consciousness was more significant than abstract thinking and intellectual logical analysis." He also said that "intuition is a very powerful thing, more powerful than intellect, in my opinion. That's had a big impact on my work."

Richard Branson, in the book *Screw It—Just Do It*, said, "I also trust my own instinct and ability to do almost anything I set my mind to. If an idea or project is good and worthwhile, if it's humanly possible, I'll always consider it seriously, even if I have never done it or thought about it before. I will never say, 'I can't do this because I don't know how to.' I'll ask people, look into it, find a way. Looking, listening, learning—these are things we should do all our lives, not just at school. Then there are those silly little rules that someone has invented for baffling reasons. I always think that if you set up quangos or committees, they will find something useless to do. The world is full of red tape, created by committees with too much time and an overbearing desire for control. Most red tape is a tangled mess of utterly useless, nonsensical jargon. If I want to do something worthwhile—or even just for fun—I won't let silly rules stop me. I will find a legal way around rules and give it a go. I tell my staff, 'If you want to do it, just do it.' That way, we all benefit."

Some people will describe intuition as a "feeling in their gut," and others will describe it as a tiny voice. Whatever it is for you is not important. What is important to understand is what ultimately happens that has a business leader and company move from more of the intuitive and become more ingrained in the logical, without even recognizing it. The answer is fear.

Throughout this book, we have discussed how convention has you believe there is a right way and a wrong way of doing everything. It is the rules and laws, and you believe that they give you a level of certainty. They make it easy to operate, because you believe you never really need to question them. If you take a look at the story of Enron or of Bernie Madoff, these are prime examples of where no one questioned what was going on. After the fact, you hear people say, "I thought something was wrong" or "my gut was telling me that something was up," but we feel protected by "the convention," so you ignore our intuition. In these two cases, they were sending out statements and filing reports, so at the surface, it had many believe everything was in order. Now of course, there are far more examples on the other side, of where businesses are in fact following the convention of business, but since there will always be these exceptions, the rules and laws are not a guarantee. This means that sometimes you do need to question what is happening around you.

One of our favorite questions in working with clients, is, "Who says?" What we find is that more times than not, it is the conventional thinking around us that we find to be behind the answer, and there are cases when it is simply wrong. There are numerous examples of where our society has held a conventional belief, later to be proven wrong. At one point, we believed that the world was flat. There was a time when we didn't believe it was possible to travel into space. For years, there were people who didn't believe it was physically possible for a person to run under a four-minute mile. We naturally build new beliefs and change old ones as you learn and grow, so it is important to question what you believe and to understand where you get your information from. Did you know that when Roger Bannister broke the four-minute mile threshold in the 1950s, a barrier the running world felt impenetrable, it was again broken twice in the following six weeks? Once you believe something is possible, it is.

As we go back in time, it is easy to find numerous examples of where individuals and companies have challenged convention, and in doing so, have created fundamental changes in a market or industry. Look at Apple and its impact on the music industry. Look at the Internet and the innovative opportunities that it provides for all entrepreneurs today. How about the innovation involved around the electronics and safety of the vehicles we drive today? As many stories as there are of innovation, there will be at least as many examples of where a person with the idea was questioned by those who hold the ideals and beliefs of convention. The difference between those who have changed the world and those who just dream about it is in their ability to address their fears.

As we have discussed, part of your filter system is made up of your beliefs and your experiences. Your thinking is constantly changing as you move through the world. As we grow up from the time we are children, we start to build and recognize patterns that allow us to delete, generalize, and distort all information that is around us in any given moment. You like to be right, and so you find the information that supports your thoughts and ideas. These patterns are mostly unconscious; however, they allow us to identify a larger picture with some accuracy, with only a little amount of detail. For example, if you look at the following, you will notice you are able to read the paragraph easily, even though it contains numerous errors:

> Aoccdrnig to rscheearch at Cmabrigde Uinervtisy, it deosn't mttaer in waht oredr the ltteers in a wrod are, the olny iprmoetnt tihng is taht the frist and lsat ltteer be at the rghit pclae. The rset can be a toatl mses and you can sitll raed it wouthit a porbelm. Tihs is bcuseae the huamn mnid deos not raed ervey lteter by istlef, but the wrod as a wlohe.

It is the pattern that your brain recognizes that allows you to read the words. It is the same principle when it comes to how you operate in the world. This same pattern recognition is what allows you to learn to drive one vehicle and apply that same knowledge to another. It is the same thing that allows us to travel around the world to different countries, without speaking the foreign language associated with those countries. It is how you learn to read, to write, and to speak. Without this amazing capability, you would not have evolved into the capable beings that we are today.

This pattern recognition plays into our intuition. As you are processing the information around you, there are times when you unconsciously notice patterns not immediately recognizable to our conscious brain. While you are unable to consciously identify the meaning of those patterns, they come into play as part of your intuition. There have been times when you have met someone new and had an immediate connection with that individual, and yet not been able to explain the connection. There have been times when you have walked into a situation and immediately felt uneasy. Upon leaving, later on you have found that something unpleasant had occurred. There are countless stories of where individuals made the decision not to get on a flight that later crashed, or all the stories of those who chose not to go into work the day of the 9/11 disaster. This is your intuition at play, and we have all had an experience where we have seen it at play. Now some of you might think, well, it is easy to put things together after the fact and notice you are right. However, more times than not, we will unconsciously say words such as, "Something just doesn't feel right," and in a moment, simply disregard the thought and carry on.

It is easy to disregard your intuition, especially when you rely on the tools of convention, those things that appear to be so logical and certain. They appear in front of you in black and white, so therefore they most certainly must be the answer. We don't know how many times we have worked with start-up companies, who have well-laid-out business plans and marketing plans, and have wondered why it is that their company has not taken off. As we start to question, we often find that, while they really wanted to start up one business, when they listened to those around them, they decided to change their minds and went in a new direction. They tell us stories about how their families didn't believe it was a good idea, or that when they went down to get a loan, the loan manager told them how risky that type of business was. They were driven to start a business, but they ignored their gut and went with what logically made sense. All the while, unconsciously, they were performing behaviors to drive them back to their original idea, even when that required the death of the current direction. We do know that in order to start and be successful in any business, you need to find your passion, because it is that passion that will have you persevere through the hard times and propel you into the good.

As you go out and experience success, you learn how to think, and the more success you have, the further it becomes ingrained in you. On the other side, when the opposite occurs, it also has an impact on how you think. You move away from what hasn't worked in the past, and even may start to reject a different type of thinking. For example, as a manager, if you have been successful in your career using logic and reasoning as the basis for what you do, then your thinking will dictate that you need an abundance of data. If as an entrepreneur, you found great success in trusting your gut, then when large sums of data are presented to you, you may very well reject them and find it to be stifling.

As we discussed in the model, it is the different types of thinking that move you naturally through the cycle; however, in order to move into a new cycle, we need to be able to increase your level of flexibility in order to counteract. While most of you will state that you are open to changing things if they are not working, it can be difficult to do so in a way that moves you far enough out of the box to see the opportunity, if you don't train your brain. As a result, you make little incremental changes, and while they may keep you busy in the busi-ness, it is often the big thinking that is required to shift the cycle.

For most business leaders, it is a type of thinking that slowly creeps in over time. As we have discussed in the model, when a leader is in the entrepreneurial phase of business, he thinks more with his gut. When he first starts out, it is like he doesn't know any better, and he is quicker on his feet. As he evolves in business, he wants to learn from some of those mistakes, because at the time they appeared to be so monumental, so he became increasingly cautious and overanalyzed. As leaders and companies continue to evolve, they become more cautious and start to rely more on logic and reason to make their business decisions. Now as we grow, this certainly makes sense, because when you think about it, if you stayed simply with the other thinking, chances are you may not exist as a company. This is the pendulum swing that we have talked about. In order to know one, you need to know the other.

The leaders who are able to keep their edge are the ones who continue to spin their company through the cycles. Those who do not, we believe, have ultimately gotten caught on one side or the other side of the thinking. If they rely solely on the logical thinking, then they become too cautious and struggle to innovate. If they rely solely on the intuitive thinking, then they may make poor business decisions. There are many companies who may have recognized this challenge and at times have brought in different executives, to counterbalance this or to take the company in a different direction. However, for most small- to medium-sized businesses, the flexibility in thinking is required by the leader in order to influence the company.

As we said earlier, the key to all of this is in being able to overcome fear. Most of you may believe that fear keeps you safe, although in fact it is our fight–or-flight response that does this. Whenever you are facing an imminent threat, there is a biological reaction in your body that takes over in order to protect you. You experience a surge of adrenaline, your blood vessels restrict, and there is more blood pumped to your muscles in the event that you need to be prepared to fight or to run away. This happens without you even thinking about it.

Fear, in fact, is constructed in your mind. Have you ever noticed that in those times when you faced and worked through an imminent threat, the fear came in afterward? It wasn't until the point that you realized how bad it could have been that you recognized that you were afraid or scared. Maybe you had a near-miss accident, and after you swerved out of the way and caught your breath, you realized how bad it all could have been. Maybe there was another time when you felt scared. In that moment, you imagined all that could have happened. Maybe you heard a noise in the house that awoke you from a deep sleep, and instantly you began to wonder if someone had broken into the house. That flight-or-fight response kicked in, and you immediately started planning your escape route or looked for something to ward off the unknown burglar, who could be there to attack or rob you. In the same way that you create problems and opportunities, we create fear. We take a present situation and we future pace it.

Now there have been numerous books and articles that have attempted to put names to the various kinds of fears. Things such as fear of success, fear of failure, fear of poverty, fear of death, fear of illness, fear of not being loved, and so on. We are sure that there is a purpose in considering different manifestations of fear; however for us, we look at fear as simply just fear. Fear relates to something that could have been or that could happen in the future, such as the worsening of a situation or continuation of a situation that is unacceptable.

We recognize that, at times, everyone feels fear, and in and of itself, it can be a great motivator. It is the fear of penalty that has you file our tax returns on time. It is the fear of punishment that has you listen to your parents. It is the fear of failure that has you try harder. In fact, in business, most of the products are sold using a form of fear. Marketing companies have used it to convince you that you need to buy whatever they are selling. Think about the commercial that depicts a person with bad breath, and as soon as they lay out that scenario, they present you with the next greatest breath mint, which will have you overcome this potential problem. They use fear in their ability to convince you that you are not complete and that you won't be perceived as successful unless you own the new vehicle. They tell us that unless you are shopping at a particular store, you won't be getting the lowest everyday prices.

Our governments and court systems use fear, in order to have you follow the laws that have been set out for a civil society. They tell you about how they are protecting you from the dangers that exist beyond our borders. They use fear to push through new laws, regulations, and budgets, convincing you there are threats just around the corner.

Our medical system has evolved to the point where they talk about preventive medicine. They tell you about the early detection of disease, and about the need to take preventive drugs and vitamins. They tell you about the signs of disease, and immediately it brings up the concern that "maybe I am sick." The pictures on the outside of cigarette packages are meant to scare you away from smoking, and the commercials on television around drunk driving are meant to remind you of the dangers on the road.

The cornerstone of much of our news and media is fear. They all know that it sells. They tell us of the tragedy and conflict that exist, and we as a society just eat it up. We like it so much, because we tell ourselves that we are okay when we can see something terrible happening to someone else. The media has news-breaking stories that influence our financial markets, that impact our thinking about the world and the economy, and they disguise it as things we all need to know. Our movies and games are filled with images that are there to frighten us. You know there is nothing better than a story where the good guy conquers the bad guy, gets the woman, and lives happily ever after. After all, an entire entertainment industry has been built on this premise, and you love to see the win of good over evil play out in front of you.

Even our nonprofit groups use it to sell their message. They talk about the risks of disease, the statistics, and the stories that scare you into believing that there are threats out there and that we all need to be vigilant because, in fact, it could happen to us. You are encouraged to give money to help find a cure "before it is too late." Think about this statement. In and of itself, what is the unconscious message to you about you? Before it is too late for whom?

We are not saying that some of this may not be real; however, at the end of the day, it is the exposure to these types of messages that begins to impact your thinking. Are there things out there people should be aware of? Absolutely. Do we all face the potential for danger? Sure, but how does that change your thinking?

Ahead of the economic crisis in the United States in 2008, the economy was booming. Housing prices were stable or growing. Companies were flourishing and exporting their goods to countries around the world, and unemployment was manageable. Now certainly, some of this had been built off a poor economic structure of overleveraging, however certainly not all of it. It could be argued that there was a switch in mind-set that set the wheels in motion and, although the government has tried to step in to ease some of the concerns, this mind-set is still there, and it continues to drive a large portion of people's behavior.

We have talked about our desire for certainty. You oftentimes let fear get in the way when you are feeling uncertain. For example, if you think about going skydiving. In order to even think about going skydiving, you need to unconsciously want to create some uncertainty, or some of you may think of this in terms of excitement. As you make your evaluations, if fear is an underlying thought, then of course you will pick up the data to support it. While you might not talk about being afraid (because rarely are we willing to admit it), you will hear about the stories where someone else was injured or about the safety record of a company or that now isn't the right time. You will make up excuses unconsciously to mask the fear. In some cases, you make up problems to mask the fear, and as we said, they become your convenient excuses. When you let the fear and excuses pile up enough, then you create certainty because by not doing anything, you have certainty in staying right where you are. What you are doing is training your mind how to think when you do this. Have you ever noticed that there are people who seem to be afraid of everything? Remember when you first started up your business, do you remember how many people tried to put their fears on you? They warned you about this and about that, but in order for you to do something different, you needed to face that fear; in doing so, you created something different for you. If you bought into the fear, you didn't. Ever notice the success or track record of those who generally warn you of all the fearful things out there?

As a business and its leader move through the cycle we discussed in the beginning chapters, the business becomes more complex, and there are more and more problems, or excuses that can mask fear. In the beginning phases, you train yourself to face fear, or simply just ignore it. At some point, generally when there is more money or employees' livelihoods are perceived to be at stake, then fear rears its head as you start trying to protect. Just in believing that you are "protecting" something, there has to be fear present, or you wouldn't feel the need to protect. Again, listen to the language in your organization. Are people talking about protecting, security, risk, safety, and so on? If that is the thinking for you or your organization and that is what they are describing as their motive for doing, it is rooted in fear.

We know that in order to overcome fear, first of all, you need to recognize and be honest with yourself that it is fear. In working with our clients, we challenge them to confront this, because once they do, then they can think in a different way. As long as they are piling up excuses, they spend more time and energy in evaluating that uncertainty, rather than creating performance. In our experience, when someone faces her fear and looks at it head-on, she will at that point see how unreal it really is and create the certainty to create momentum. Just think for a moment about sometime when you really wanted to do something, and you admitted that you were afraid. At that moment, if that was the only thing you faced, you pushed through and did it. You said to yourself, "I can do this," and you did. It is always easier when you are dealing with one thing, rather than being overwhelmed by all the excuses.

So, let's recap the thinking that we have been talking about in this chapter. First of all, there are some beliefs that we encourage you to adopt, right now:

- In order to lead, you need to have both logical and intuitive thinking; otherwise, you are not leading, you are managing.
- Fear is constructed in your mind. It is a message that you are focusing on what could go wrong, rather than what could go right.
- If you admit to fear, then you can face it and move forward. You are training your mind how you want it to think. You are in charge of your thinking.

Remember fear can be a great motivator, and it is used all around you in order to have you take the action that someone or some group wants you to take. At its essence, this is how we create demand for the products and services we sell. As soon as people are afraid they will miss out, or something bad will happen, or there will be a penalty, or they will fail, or they will die, and such, then they get certain in your product or service and they take action. As cruel as this may sound, it is a part of the game, and it is played all over. Now of course, your product or service is filling a need in an ecological way, however don't fool yourself into thinking that fear isn't still at play. Even when you tell yourself your customers really want your product or service, it is because they are afraid of the consequences, whether real or not, on the other side.

However for you, if you allow fear and all the excuses to freeze you up, then you will not take the action required to continue to strengthen your company. The next time you consider that you want to do something (take on a big project, introduce a new product line, etc.), consider taking the following steps and recognize that you are training your mind to think in a different way:

- Get clear on what you are considering doing. It helps to write this down, at least initially.

- Admit that in the uncertainty, you have fear.
  - o Write down what you are specifically afraid of. For example:
    - I am afraid of failing and letting people down.
    - I am afraid of overleveraging the company.
    - I am afraid of not being able to secure labor resources.
  - o Now take each of these fears separately, and ask yourself whether they are even possible, recognizing that you know they are possible. What we mean is, for example:
    - Is it possible that you could intentionally fail or let people down, based on what you know of you and your team?
    - Is it possible that you could intentionally overleverage the company?
    - Is it possible that you could not be able to secure labor resources?

    In this step, you will notice some of these will immediately fall out because of what you know about you and your team. For example, you will know there is no way you would intentionally let anyone down or fail and that you have proven over and over that you have what it takes to be successful. The same could be said for overleveraging your company. You will know what you are comfortable with, and you will know that you will set the parameters of the project based on that. In this step you are recovering your skills, resources, and thinking that has made you successful, and you will realize that sure, this is possible (you can make up anything in our minds), but based on what you know, this isn't enough to stop you.
  - o For any fears that remain, just put in place a plan to resolve them, based on what you know. Focus stubbornly on the question, "How can I do this?" You will immediately have some thoughts on what you can do to resolve the fear. Most importantly, define the first step and take action on it right away. As soon as the first step falls into place, the fear will disappear, and you will be certain on what you are doing.

With work and guidance, it is possible to rid yourself completely of fear. Look around the world at the biggest and most influential people you can think of. Ask yourself, are they fearful? Our guess is no, and we know there are a special class of individuals who literally are free of this disempowering emotion. We can only stress to you the importance of removing and working through your fears, as we have outlined or through any way that presents itself. Your investment in this will change your thinking in ways that are unfathomable to you today.

Holding Your Intention

Throughout the years, in coaching people and executives, we have marveled at one simple point. Many people have no idea what they really want. When we first meet a new client, he will tell us what he doesn't want, and by his simply making these statements, we know that he already has that. He will tell us he doesn't want to work long hours. He will tell us he doesn't want to work with customers with whom he doesn't feel aligned. He will tell us he doesn't want to do things for nothing. Just from these statements, we know he is working long hours, working with customers whom he is not aligned with, and charging clients nothing for doing it.

You can't know what you don't want unless that is exactly what you have. It is the way it works. It is really that simple. We will ask the client again, what is it that you want, and oftentimes, while she might start out and tell us one or two things that are in that direction, before long she will slip back into the other side and again tell us what she doesn't want. You can get a lot of information from people on what they have simply by listening to what they don't want.

In order to achieve anything, you need to know what it is you want; however, this is generally a tough question for business leaders, for companies, and for individuals to answer. Children, when they are young, say around two, start to ask for what it is they want. In fact, around that age, they are funny, as they are incredibly resourceful in getting what they want, whether that is a toy, getting attention, or staying up late. It doesn't matter. They know what they want, and they will do whatever it takes to get it, or until you outlast them as a parent. They will ask nicely, and then they will demand, they will even throw themselves on the floor with a temper tantrum. This is one side of the pendulum.

In order to break this pattern, parents and teachers start to teach their children when it is appropriate to ask for what you want, and before long, children know that it is okay to ask for something to eat when they are hungry. They learn there is a rule about when they are to go to bed. They learn that when Sally is playing with a toy, they need to wait until she is done to play with it. They learn that if they want to speak up in class, they need to put their hand up, and at some appropriate time, they will be called upon to talk. This is part of how you evolve in our society; however, through this process, you start to learn not to ask for what you want or desire. You learn about convention and the rules, and these can limit you if you never ask the question "Who says?"

As you enter into your teenage years, you are full of hopes and dreams, and as you talk about them, you start to listen to the opinions of your peers, your society, and your families, and their opinions creep into the mix. While you might have believed that you want to write lyrics for songs, you have those around you who know nothing about whether that might or might not be possible, tell you that "there are very few people in this world who have the talent to do that; you need to be more reasonable." On some level, you choose to accept or not accept that belief, and if you do accept it, then you learn that while you might really want to do something, there are limitations, based on convention.

As you finish school and maybe go on to postsecondary education, you learn there is a right way and a wrong way to do everything, whether that is in business, engineering, a laboratory, or law. You learn the convention of your trade, and as you mix with your peers, you start to build your own ideas of what success will look like. There is a path you need to follow, and everyone knows that if you get a job with XYZ firm, then you will be successful. Right? Have you ever thought that?

Every once in a while, there will be someone who decides—generally early on—he is not going to buy into any of this. He is going to live life his own way, and he is going to do what he is going to do. In school, he might have been the boy who spent a lot of time in the principal's office. Chances are that if he went to university, he dropped out before too long. He was the person who, in spite of what everyone else said, was going to do what he wanted to do, and as long as he hung onto that conviction, chances are he did it.

It is not uncommon to see this early on with young adults, but they lose this once the other priorities of life slowly creep in. They buy a house, they get married, and they have kids. At that point, some of their drive diminishes, due to the loss of focus or the focus on other things that are more important to them. There are certainly cases where they are able to balance this, depending on their relationships with the people closest to them. As parents, at some unconscious level, you probably understand this. Many parents will encourage their children not to get married too early, or to go and explore the world, or to be open to different types of work, depending on their own beliefs around what creates success. There are very few people who believe you can have it all, and in having that belief, you become afraid of going after it all.

People often don't know what they want because what happens is that they let doubt and fear get in the way. They don't dream, because you just don't feel it's possible. We have discussed that, whether it is a problem or an opportunity, you construct these in a way that hinge multiple things or ideas on top of each other. For example, you might want to have a million dollars, but behind the scenes, you have thoughts that make it seem impossible to obtain that. Thoughts like, you don't know how you would do that or what could create that. What would that mean in regard to the time you would need to spend in order to get that? What if you failed? So with these ideas playing out behind the scenes, when you talk about the million dollars, you struggle to build the certainty that gives you the momentum to drive toward that goal.

Secondly, you are afraid to ask for what we want. It is something that you knew how to do when you were young, but over time, a large percentage of people feel bad about asking for what they want. It has been ingrained in you from a very young age. You are told over and over again when it is appropriate to ask. Again, fear comes into play. Thoughts like "What would they think of me?" "What if they said no?" "What would that say about me?" "I couldn't do that!" People who are great at doing sales, and please notice, we said great at sales, have learned to overcome this. They understand that even in the word no lies the opportunity to find a yes, if they can just address the objection. If you want to have success in anything, you need to get comfortable asking for what you want, and then knowing that even if you get a no, there is always another way.

The third thing is that people underestimate what is possible, because you don't have the certainty you need to believe it is possible in order to take action. This is where fear comes into play. If you see a mistake as failure and you have fear of failure, then of course, you are going to do everything you can to ensure that you don't do things that could be construed as a mistake, or which lead to a mistake. If on the other hand, you regard a mistake as nothing and simply see it as something that you learned, then you don't let it define you and you continue on. There are so many people who are afraid of making a mistake. In reality, all of us have done so. You certainly didn't see it as such when you went in, but unfortunately or fortunately, you don't live our lives in reverse.

A mistake, again, is simply a construction in your mind, and it always happens after the fact, as you make your evaluation of the situation. Even if you plan to make a mistake, it then cannot in fact be a mistake, although that may be the word you use to describe it. When you plan to do something, it becomes an intention. We believe everything we or you do has a positive intention for us in any given moment. We act, in any given moment; based on the information you have available at the time. Sometimes maybe you don't have all of the information, and at other times, how you are filtering information can be skewed one way or another, but we are acting with the best intention for you. Now, please understand it may not have a positive intention for someone else or for something else, but moment to moment, you all do what we believe to be correct for you.

After the fact is when the evaluation comes into play, and as you do this analysis, you give it the label. Let us say, you added up a column of numbers wrong, having not noticed that you transposed one of the numbers in the process. In the moment when you were adding the numbers, you didn't think you were making a mistake. You may not have even immediately recognized what you did. It wasn't until later, when you recognized something didn't look right, you realized what you had done, through the analysis of the situation. Now, did you mean to do that? No, you were just carrying out a process, and after the fact you recognized the error and labeled it as a mistake.

Now, sometimes you carry out actions and in doing so; understand they may have a negative impact on someone else. Before you take those actions, there is a split-second evaluation of the situation, and you make a decision to do what you think is best for you. You may even recognize in the end, you may have to make amends, but in that moment, you balance the odds and do what you believe to be the best for you. In our training, we will often have those who ask, well, what about someone who kills someone else? Even in this case, the person will have taken action based on what she believed was best for her in the situation. It could have been she thought that she might be harmed or she was protecting someone. It could have been she wanted something, and a person was in the way from her getting it. Whatever the explanation after the fact, at some point, she carried out her actions based on the best information she had available for her in that moment. Sure, after the fact, she may see her actions as a mistake, once the repercussions of her actions come into play, but at the time, she was doing what she consciously or unconsciously believed to be the best alternative. This comes back to the cause and effect equation. If you believe you are at cause for everything you do, then you can go on and create something different. You are in charge of your thinking, and therefore your results.

The concept that you construct mistakes is important to understand, because in many ways, it clouds your thinking in terms of what you want. Many people will beat themselves up over and over for the things that have happened to them. They tell themselves that they shouldn't have done this, and they shouldn't have done that. In fact, all around, you are bombarded by people telling each other exactly the same thing. Now, we understand that all of this is with good intention; however, how you talk to yourself does impact your psyche, over time.

Earlier, we discussed briefly the reason we never ask a person "Why?" This is it. More times than not, he really has no idea, so it really is a pointless question, if in fact you are working to create something different. We believe that you get what you focus on. If you are focusing on the reasons, then you will never find results.

Now, you may believe that we are crazy, and in fact, maybe we are. We hold a belief that everything happens for a reason and there is no such thing as "mistakes." If everyone is doing the best they can do with the information they have available at the time, then really how can that be possible? In fact, we prefer our clients take the word out of their vocabulary, because there really is no such thing. This is a label that has been created in order to let people off the hook when they are asked the question "Why?" How many times have you heard someone ask, "Why did you do that?" and the answer is, "Sorry about that, it was a mistake."

The second thing around the word itself is that if you break it down into its parts, it is *mis take*, or *miss* and then *take*. What does that mean? We believe the language you unconsciously use describes how you see the world that you live in. As we discussed earlier, at the same time you are saying anything, there are images and sounds being played through our minds, constructing what you believe to be reality. If you look down at your watch and you realize you are late for a meeting, for an instant, what may flash through your mind is the meeting room you are going to, you may get images of the people who will be attending, you may play through an important thing you need to remember, or you may see the agenda that is sitting on your desk. Outwardly, all you may be saying to someone else is, "I have to go" or "I will be late for a meeting." Again, this is how you process your world.

The words we use hold meaning in your minds. Back to the word *miss take*. What does that bring to mind? While this may be different for you, for us it implies that, while I had a positive intention for me in the action that I took, I was wrong in carrying it out, for me. The more times I tell myself this, over a period of time, unconsciously, I train myself to know that anything I may think I want would be a miss. Have you ever noticed that once someone gets herself on the "mistake train," in a short period of time, she just seems to create more? Recognize, that you *miss took* the information you had in that moment. You were carrying out what you believed to be the correct action in that specific moment, and if you had had other information, chances are you would have done something different, wouldn't you have? People have a tendency to live in the past and beat themselves up, although you will agree you can never go back. Living in the past is just avoiding the future.

We encourage our clients to become conscious of the language they are using, especially if they are the leader of an organization. Another example is the word "know." Now on the surface, we all understand that according to the dictionary, "know" means to hold information in mind or to be certain of something, to realize something, or to comprehend something. When you see that in writing, you get that; however, how is that different from the word "no", when you hear it? How many times have you heard someone say to you, "I know," and immediately it brings into question in your mind that maybe they don't? It is a tricky one, because when you say the words, you understand what they mean, but in this simple word, it can place a doubt in the other person. If you haven't noticed this, just become aware of what happens when you hear, "I know," when someone says it to you.

One of the questions we will often ask people is whether they would talk to a small child the way that they talk to themselves, and most of the time, they say no. Most of us wouldn't tell a small child he was stupid, or lazy, or ugly; and yet, you will tell yourself those types of things over and over throughout the day. The language you use does, in fact, influence how you see and interpret the world. You need to be purposeful in what you are saying, and again, it needs to be focused on what you want.

As we said earlier, it is amazing how many people don't know what they, themselves, want. When we ask them the question, the second thing we check for is whether or not it is they who really want whatever they are telling us. As we go into businesses, it is not uncommon to hear leaders talk about what they have been told they should want; however, in this, they are not necessarily clear on the purpose or the intention behind it.

Not that long ago, we worked with a company, and when we asked the owner what he wanted, he told us that he was implementing a new compensation system, which included a bonus structure for staff. As he described the project, it became evident there was some disagreement taking place in terms of the direction it was going. His staff wanted to implement a points system that would drive the bonus structure, while he thought it was going to create a lot of work and he wasn't sure that it was necessary. We asked him the purpose and intention in doing this, and he told us his Human Resource Department had told him that in order to retain his staff, he really needed to make this change. We respected there was a reason that he had decided to explore this; however, it was unclear whether he wanted to, or whether he believed that he *should* "want to" do this. As we dug a little deeper, it became evident that it was the latter. He didn't believe there was a retention issue with his staff. He felt that, in fact, it was the opposite. He knew he had retained staff in the past based on, not only what he paid them, but on having a shared vision, on making work fun, and how he involved his people. As we continued to talk through the issue, he realized that, in fact, he really didn't believe it was necessary.

So, how did this play out in the thinking of his organization? First of all, it changed his focus. He said that as soon as the issue came up, he began to recognize that losing staff was a possibility, and he started to see his employees in a different way. He became concerned about what would happen if someone were to leave and started making plans in case it was to happen. Secondly, because unconsciously he wasn't fully behind the idea, he recognized even though his staff was coming up with solutions, he was too busy unconsciously looking for the reasons why whatever they were coming up with wouldn't work. This created disagreement between him and his human resource staff, and he recognized he had created a situation where he had planted a level of doubt into their abilities. Finally, he realized that having this conflicting focus, both in him and his staff, had taken away from what it was important to focus on. He said that the process had taken some of the fun out of the organization, which was key in why people stayed there in the first place.

He once again focused on his intention for the company and for his staff. He became clear on how he could create that, without buying into the idea of implementing a new compensation system. He engaged his human resource staff in coming up with new ways to leverage what was important in their culture, and the focus and fun that were so important to their success were regained. It was an incredible learning experience for him to be clear on what he wanted and to be cautious about buying into the things that others wanted to believe that he should want.

If there is only one point that you take from this book, here it is: *Get clear on your intention and focus on what you want.*

Now on the other side of the coin, we will have people ask us about planning for the risks that come in running a business. They will say, "How about if I decide to go into a new venture, or to expand my business, shouldn't I be looking at the risks?" Well, of course you should; however, you need to be able to understand if they are real, and the only way that you can do this is by truly understanding your intention.

The first thing to understand about risks is that you are making them up. As we said before, none of you really knows what is going to happen in the next five minutes, never mind a year from now. One of our favorite things is when individuals tell us that there are statistics available to support their thinking. It was Mark Twain who said, "There are three kinds of lies: lies, damned lies, and statistics." We believe this to be true, especially today, with the availability of information via the Internet.

We would argue that based on how you naturally process information, almost all of your thinking is deductive in nature. This means that you come up with an idea and then you go off and find information that supports what you believe to be true. If you think about it, you learned this in school in the science lab. Remember doing those experiments where you were proving a hypothesis, and as part of the lab, you defined the proof? Think back to the science fair project, where you might have wanted to prove that by talking to one set of bean plants, they would grow faster than the ones you didn't talk to. In order to set up the experiment, you needed to determine what it was you were going to prove or disprove, before you got started, and then you went about collecting information that supported it either way.

Most of our science has been built the same way. We hypothesize something, such as, I believe if we add this compound to this one, then it will cure cancer. Then we go about collecting data to prove it one way or the other. As you learn more, you make variations; however, you work to prove out your theories. If you read history books from different countries on the same war conflict, it is pretty common to see entirely different perspectives and beliefs about what, in fact, took place. If one country believes it won, then its history tells the story of everything it did right to accomplish that and what its opponent did wrong. The other country, even if they lost, will believe it won something, and its history will tell the story of what it did right to get that. If you look at this, you even go about this in how you justify to others that which you want to or don't want to do. If you decide that you want to leave the office for the day to go golfing, you will justify it by saying you came into work early, you are the boss, you will be discussing a business deal. Whatever you tell yourself, you are using deductive thinking to prove your hypothesis.

Statistics are the same thing. Anytime someone is putting together statistics, they inherently have to find data to support their case. They then use that data to back up their own arguments. We cannot tell you how many investment opportunities people have pitched to us that on the surface appeared to have incredible business plans to back them up, but in the end didn't hold water. This is one of the pitfalls of many start-up businesses. They are unclear about their intention to get into business. They come up with an idea, and then they go about proving exactly what they want, without really understanding what they bring to the table to make that happen. They write the plan and believe, because it looks good on paper, then it will be a success, without really thinking about where they are getting the data from. Is it their thought and knowledge, or are they relying on someone else's thinking, without really knowing what that someone else was really thinking? Were they clear of focus and intention?

If you are ever looking to have some fun in your spare time, pick a topic like global warming and go see how much information you can find on the topic. Then do the same for global cooling. You will find supposed competing facts and data, and you may even find that the same data have been used, although interpreted in a different way.

In fact, we are so clear on this point that we know there will be some of you who, in reading this, will believe that we must be wrong and may want to prove it. We think you should, if that is where you want to focus your energy. The only thing we will ask you is whether or not what you have been doing is working for you. If it has, please keep doing what you are doing; however, if not, be open to seeing and thinking about the world differently and notice the difference it will make for you and your company.

To recognize the impact of a risk, you need to be clear on what you have right now, right in front of you, and what it is you have a focus and intention of creating. As we look into different investments, we always evaluate them based on what we know in the here and now. We certainly evaluate the potential, but we look at the strength we have today, which may or may not be required to capture that opportunity. Remember we focus on what we want, and while there are those who talk about understanding their weaknesses, we know you need to be clear on the resources you can bring to bear when the need arises. This is one of the key reasons we discussed the need for surrounding yourself with the best. In your hiring practices, if you only hire mediocre, then that is what you have to bring to bear. If in your networks, you only surround yourself with people like you, then that is what you have to bring to bear. If in your company, you don't buy the best tools for the job, then that is what you have to bring to bear. If you have overextended yourself in not managing your cash flow, then that is what you have to bring to bear. If you know absolutely nothing about a new industry, then that is what you bring to bear. All of this needs to be considered, and this is where you need to make the change in order to go after something new. All of this is within your control, and as you invest in strengthening this, everything becomes solvable.

This brings us back to, what is your intention? What are you focused on? As a leader, the clearer you are, the easier it all becomes in leading your company. It comes out in your language, and the people around you being able to hear you in a different way. They learn to know what is important and what isn't, and their actions will come in to support you in a way you couldn't have imagined. It comes out in the opportunities that you will begin to notice around you. You truly recognize the strength we have as individuals and as an organization to take on those bigger challenges, because the answers are clearer.

We know that along the way, there will be things that will attempt to pull you off course. What we say is that the only time you run into these things is when you are moving, and the only time they will pull you off course is when you are not clear on where you are going. Think about a time when you had to get someplace, and something happened that could have gotten in your way. Now, you could have focused on the "problem," but you kept your focus on the outcome, and because you did so, you came up with a solution. You do this all the time when you are clear on what you really want; however, when you get into business, sometimes you forget how easy it can really be. Instead, you get focused on the day-to-day stuff and make it difficult.

So, let's recap the thinking we have been talking about in this chapter. First of all, there are some beliefs that we encourage you to adopt, right now:

- In order to know where you are going, you need to get clear on what *you* want.
    o If you are describing your world based on what you don't want, then know that you already have that and get clear on what you do want.
    o Be clear on what you want, and watch for the cases where you are in a "want to want" situation. When you find those, get clear on what you want and either get behind it or stop it.
- The only chance you have to get what you want is to ask for it. Even if you get a no, recognize that you just need to answer the objection, and once you do, then it will turn into a yes.

Begin to recognize the language you are using each and every day and the language that is being used by your employees in your organization. What is consuming the focus and the energy? The more energy you can direct toward what you want, the faster you will be able to take on new opportunities.

Get clear on building a strong resource base and team for yourself. Recognize you can overcome any risk, as long as you have the tools in place to do so and as long as you are realistic about the strengths you can bring to bear. Surround yourself with people who think differently and in doing so, create different results.

Once you are clear on your intentions, you need to focus diligently on your success, realizing that while other things may try to pull you off course, the only chance they have to do so is if you waver. We will always be challenged in our conviction about what we want. If you see these challenges as brick walls, they will in fact stop you. If you see them as bridges, they will carry you over the traffic to the other side.

Conclusion

In making it to this point, you realize the unreal parts of convention and supposed rules out there in the world. You will now realize we were correct when we said at the beginning, "We believe success in business or in anything is simply all in your mind." Remember in the introduction when we challenged you to write down your thoughts around business? As you look at those now, you notice you have had a dramatic shift in your thinking. In knowing that, you also realize you are firmly on the path that, if you choose to continue on, will enable you to create success for you and your organization.

As you read the book, you will begin to notice and consider things that seemed "real" to you previously, and now you will see them differently. In this, we are guessing that many of the rules that fit only a short time ago no longer make sense to you. Or perhaps you find yourself questioning the things around you and find you are unsure of what to believe in some areas. This is a great indicator of your shift in thinking! Remember, uncertainty creates new growth in thinking, and that is what we have endeavored to do here. To create uncertainty, you must question, and questioning brings in new ideas for growth. Through the uncertainty, you will be creating new rules and ideas that support you in your quest. Embrace the uncertainty, break it down, and realize that in the reconstruction, you always have the possibility of focusing on something different, and in doing so, creating something different.

We know you will have become openly aware of your thinking from moment to moment. Remember, your thinking at any point is a reflection of you only in that moment. As we discussed, in any moment, you can be on the cause side of the equation, or you can be at effect to your own thinking and believe that everything is out of control. You are in charge of your thinking, so in each moment, make the choice to be at cause and be expansive.

There will be times when you may fall off your horse; however, success comes from how fast you get up, find a horse of a different color, and get back on. Those who sit on the ground waiting for the horse to pick them up have to wait a long time and end up being trampled. We have said over and over, truly adapting this style of thinking is not for everyone. Look around at the herd. Some awaken for periods, only to find themselves falling back into the issues of the day to day, and they go back to sleep.

Your thinking and results are impacted by the environment that you choose to be a part of, so please choose wisely. Look for environments and people who will challenge you to continue on this path. Challenge yourself to continue growing and learning. As we have demonstrated, those who do remain innovative continually refresh themselves and their thinking, and they are able to hold an intention that allows them to work the cycles. They continue to create possibility and to see the opportunities that allow them to let something die, so that something else can live and flourish. We know today, you are noticing cycles within your company or organization, and you will notice others are completely asleep to them. Remember to hold your focus and intention, be expansive in your thinking, and know that you get what you give.

Today, knowing what you know, you know convention remains all around us, bound by the societal buy-in; however, it can be useful when you understand what it really is. Just this premise alone opens the door to creating what you want to create as a leader. So, be a little crazy, and go that extra mile. Stare down the convention and ask the question "Who says?" There are numerous examples of where people have gone out on a limb, and in doing so, have fundamentally changed convention and the world:

- IBM, in the 1970s, ridiculed the idea that computers would ever be small enough or affordable enough to be contained in every home and office and yet not a decade later, there was the introduction of the Commodore 64.
- John Baird, in 1924, offered the viewing of the first television system to the Royal Society (British scientists). They scoffed and ridiculed it.
- C. J. Doppler, in 1842, proposed the theory of the optical Doppler effect, but was bitterly opposed for two decades because it did not fit with the accepted physics of the time. Doppler was finally

proven correct in 1868, when W. Huggins observed red shifts and blue shifts in stellar spectra—proving the abilities of the Doppler radar system. Unfortunately for Doppler, this was fifteen years after his death.

- Galileo was scoffed at by his fellow scientists about the telescope and criticized for his claims. They did so, saying they would only see what he said because he bewitched them. Galileo and his claim that our earth circled the sun were violently rejected by the world.

Remember, the premise of convention creates intention that is deductive in nature. In school, you are taught to pick an end point or hypothesis and to then go about proving it to be right. Now, when you pick your end points, evaluate your intention and notice whether your intention is to grow and expand, or protect and contract.

From here on in, when you pick an end point, pick an amazing one and be open to the tools and resources that are in front of you in this moment that will assist you to accomplish it. It is easy to fall into the logical and methodical analysis of things based on the rules of convention, and at times this may even be important. However, equally as important is the knowing in your "gut," as often intuition is the thinking that has you take a leap of faith. Intuition is you being in tune to the cycles, the understanding of whether you are fighting a headwind or catching a wave. It is the thing that gets you excited and motivated, knowing deep down that you have the passion to make it work. Those firmly aligned have uncanny abilities to understand intuitively when rules need to be broken; we call these "paradigm shifters."

The law of requisite variety as captured in systems theory states that the person or thing with the most flexibility in a system, in fact controls the system. As a leader, you need to be the most flexible, and that flexibility comes from how you interpret the world around you. Remember the only thing you can be certain of is there will be uncertainty. When we are certain, we take action; however, most people spend a lot of time and energy in the uncertainty. They look for us to climb in the boat with them. They try to prepare themselves for the worst case. They make up reasons and excuses. They find problems. They let the fear of the uncertainty overtake what they know of themselves. You have an amazing amount of skills and resources available to you, and as you now realize, anytime you have had to face a situation, you have worked through it once we got started. Remember that much of the uncertainty is a construction, and as you know now, you can only do this by future pacing something in the here and now. You are making it up, and so we will say, if you are making it up, then make up what you want. You as a leader must be willing to outflex your environment. You need to recover quickly, to stay on message, to match your words with your actions, and to hold a higher intention for you and your company. Many may disagree with your directions and ideas—after all, you will be working with the tides, whereas the herd wants to fight the tides. Be patient, allow things to die that should, and breathe life into those ideas and products with merit.

It is easy to live in dichotomy, where there is good or bad, right or wrong, this or that. This is certainty. This is the thinking that has you fall asleep. Is there always a right or a wrong? You know if this were in fact the case, there would be no such thing as gray. Challenge your thinking by living in paradox. When is something neither right nor wrong? When is something not broken but rather it is fixed? We have all heard of the things that proved to be something even better when they were thought to be broken. Chances are you have a Post-It note on your desk. Wasn't it broken to start with?

We have told you over and over, your organization is a reflection of your thinking as a leader. If you want to make a change, create that change inside yourself, and watch the change trickle through the organization. You get what you give, and it starts inside. You are the most powerful projector in your organization; own that power, and own that responsibility. Take it seriously and commit to continuing to expand your thinking. Your organization and employees will follow you anywhere when you do.

Just in reading this book, we know that you know, you have started making changes in your own thinking, and in many cases, you are beginning to see those changes manifest. As always, coupled with this, your physiological state controls your thinking. Always know that when you are in a powerful, resourceful state, you are able to handle any challenge with ease. When you want powerful thinkers inside your organization, then you need to be powerful in your resolve to stay focused and hold your intention around what you want for you and remain in that powerful state. You are in charge of your thinking. You decide how you are going to feel about something. You decide how you are going to react. You are in charge.

You will run into people who will tell you that you are wrong. We do. They tell us their business and their organization is different. They tell us their problem is bigger and we don't understand. Remember, new ideas and new thinking require the person to have an open mind. We know that people, while brilliant and resourceful, can find change difficult when they are "certain" of something to the contrary. It is from going through a period of uncertainty, that they find the certainty that gives them the momentum to make the change. Arthur Schopenhauer, an influential philosopher in the nineteenth century, wrote about truth and ideas and how they go through three stages. In the first, they are ridiculed; in the second, they are violently rejected; and in the third stage, they are finally considered self-evident.

Even as we were presenting a model of thinking in relation to the business and product life cycles, we acknowledged that this was also a convention. Could it be wrong? Absolutely. However, we know you recognize that when a leader or an organization is asleep to the cycles and swings that are just part of nature, they have no choice but to follow it. In your case, you have now been awakened to this, so of course we would expect you will create something different for you. We expect you will see the cycles and that you will be aware of the swings. We know you will see where the certainty and uncertainty exist, and you will notice the behaviors that occur as a result. We know you have changed your thinking, and if you have pieced it together for you, then you will have different results. It may take some time. You may have to read over sections of the book again. You may seek additional tools and resources, and commit to refreshing yourself as a leader. You may find others to share this thinking with, but remember that you can't un-know, something you know. Now that you know what you know, it is up to you to take action and to create the results we know you are capable of achieving.

In just knowing what you know, you have now crossed a bridge, entering a world where sometimes it is a little lonely. The people living in this world are different from the herd, and sometimes, they can appear to be a "little crazy" compared to the norm. As the late Steve Jobs was famous for pointing out, those who changed the world were the ones who were crazy enough to believe they could. Would you prefer the path less taken, the one with results? You have only stepped to the edge of a bridge, where new thinking and creation is the norm. Will you continue to grow and challenge yourself beyond the edge to cross that bridge, or will you go back to the convention and certainty? We offer guidance to our students and clients that often the path they are embarking on is exciting, and one of great reward and creation. As you begin to see and experience the benefits, you will want to share. As you do, know that you are on the path less taken, and initially the herd may buck your ideas. Let your performance and creation speak for themselves. People become curious as you create success, and at this point, they begin to ask questions. As curiosity rises, you will have opportunity to offer your new ways of thinking. Remember that:

> "Men show their character in nothing more clearly than by what they think laughable." —J. W. Goethe

You will have clear ideas and notions on where your business is sitting and where your thinking is today. Remember, your thinking is a snapshot in time. You can choose to change it, grow, evolve, and develop. After all, we were meant to. As you think about your organization and about yourself as a leader, you may be wondering, can I do more? Can I accelerate this thinking? Of course, do whatever you can to immerse yourself in it every day. If you are wondering where to go from here, ask yourself four simple questions in regard to getting on the expansive-thinking path:

- What will happen if you do become expansive in your thinking?
- What will happen if you don't become expansive in your thinking?
- What won't happen if you don't become expansive in your thinking?
- What won't happen if you do become expansive in your thinking?

Take each question, take time, and really think through the questions. We promise you will find new certainty in your need to not take action or to take action. You will see new motivation and insight into moving forward and the possibilities that will result through such action. As these questions offer clarity to you and your perception of the need to move forward, be curious of the avenues around you to accelerate your thinking and progress. What sources can you find to assist you? Who around you "gets it" that you can spend time with? What are you missing from your company that would assist you in creating the intentions and vision necessary to create and maintain an expansive culture?

Back to the story about reducing our cycle time from twenty-four days to three. I knew that I didn't have the answers. I was scared about what everyone around me was going to think of me as a leader. As I went out and told my three hundred staff people that this was what we were going to achieve, it surprised me that there was actually a buzz of excitement. They knew that it was different. They knew it was going to take all of us to think differently about what it was we were doing. It was going to require us to question everything we thought we knew about making airplane parts, and it was going to require us all to work together. You know, one of the things that I am so proud about, is that hanging on the wall in my office is a shadow box with a Lacrosse pen and pencil set. Each day, I look up at it and remind myself that amazing things can happen when you believe that they can.

I am grateful for Bill and everything he taught me. He didn't teach me about building an airplane part, or how to use this tool or that tool. He pushed me, and in doing so, changed my thinking. He taught me, by example, what it truly means to lead and what it means to overcome the fear of uncertainty. He held such a high intention for all of us there was no way we couldn't succeed. You see, Bill thought differently and demonstrated firsthand what miraculous things occur when you hold a higher intention inside an organization. It is an important lesson that has allowed us to continue to create performance in a different way.

We hold the intention for you as you grow as a leader that you will find your Bill, and create your bridge to new and expansive thinking in your organization. Remember, you get what you give.

End Notes

1 Small Business Information Needs Assessment Survey, Government of Canada, http://www.ic.gc.ca/eic/site/061.nsf/eng/rd00082.html, modified May 2012.

2 Capobiano, Robert. "Accolade Opens New Office To Support Growth" http://www.marketwatch.com/story/accolade-opens-new-office-to-support-growth-2012-08-16, August 2012.

3 Research in Motion (USA) Annual Data, Google Finance, http://www.google.ca/finance?q=NASDAQ:RIMM&fstype=ii, August 2012.

4 Research in Motion (USA) Quarterly Data, Google Finance, http://www.google.ca/finance?q=NASDAQ:RIMM&fstype=ii, August 2012.

5 Research in Motion CEO Provides Business Update, http://finance.paidcontent.org/about/news/read/21448315/research_in_motion_ceo_provides_business_update, May 2012.

6 Bernnard, Molly et al:, Turnaround Management, Columbia Business School, http://turnaround.org/cmaextras/CROX---Carl-Marks-Case-Study.pdf, April 2012.

7 "Crocs IPO Takes Off," *Denver Business Journal*, http://www.bizjournals.com/denver/stories/2006/02/06/daily36.html, February 8, 2006.

8 Crocs, Inc (USA) Annual Data, Google Finance, http://www.google.com/finance?q=NASDAQ:CROX&fstype=ii, August 2012.

9 Research in Motion (USA) Quarterly Data, Google Finance, http://www.google.ca/finance?q=NASDAQ:RIMM&fstype=ii, August 2012.

About the Photographer

Hailing from the north shores of Thunder Bay, Ontario, born and raised in Brandon, Manitoba, I've been fortunate enough to be exposed to some of the most beautiful landscapes and waterscapes Canada has to offer. I attribute my passion for photography and desire to have ever picked up a camera to where I live.

I'm a self-taught photographer, a lover of nature, and a willing explorer. I've spent countless early mornings, alone, combing the shores of Lake Superior for photo opportunities, while most were still home in bed. Sometimes I come back empty-handed, but sometimes I am lucky enough to capture breath-taking sunrises.

Life, like photography, has its up and downs, a lot of it stems from being in the right place at the right time, but without the skills, those opportunities are often missed. Practice and dedication have given me the knowledge to take advantage of these moments.

For those reading this, thanks for your time, I know it is precious and I hope I didn't waste it.

To view more of my work, search "Trevor Anderson Photography" (from Thunder Bay) on Facebook and www.flickr.com

Thank You,
Trevor Anderson